The RADIANT LIVES
of ANIMALS

THE RADIANT LIVES
OF ANIMALS

LINDA HOGAN

BEACON PRESS
Boston

BEACON PRESS
Boston, Massachusetts
www.beacon.org

Beacon Press books
are published under the auspices of
the Unitarian Universalist Association of Congregations.

23 22 21 20   8 7 6 5 4 3 2 1

This book is printed on acid-free paper that meets the uncoated paper
ANSI/NISO specifications for permanence as revised in 1992.

Text design by Louis Roe
Typesetting by Kim Arney
Cover and interior illustrations by James Blackburn

"Dawn for All Time" was previously published in *Yes Magazine*. "The Great Without"
was first published in *Parabola* 24:1 (Spring 1999). "The Radiant Life with Animals" was
previously published in *Earth Island Journal*.

Library of Congress Cataloging-in-Publication Data

Names: Hogan, Linda, author.
Title: The radiant lives of animals / Linda Hogan.
Description: Boston : Beacon Press, [2020]
Identifiers: LCCN 2020011365 (print) | LCCN 2020011366 (ebook) | ISBN 9780807047927
    (hardcover ; acid-free paper) | ISBN 9780807047989 (ebook)
Subjects: LCSH: Human-animal relationships.
Classification: LCC PS3558.O34726 A6 2020 (print) | LCC PS3558.O34726 (ebook) |
    DDC 811/.54—dc23
LC record available at https://lccn.loc.gov/2020011365
LC ebook record available at https://lccn.loc.gov/2020011366

CONTENTS

PREFACE

The Great Without

In European natural histories, human imagination was most often projected onto the outside world. Pliny's *Natural History*, for instance, was a false map of our true American continent, where dog-headed humans could only bark, people had heads in their chests, and others had only one foot but the ability to leap powerfully and also to use the large foot like a tree for shade. Mermaids surfaced in rivers and oceans. Springs were believed to grant eternal life, and demons or angels inhabited islands. Bestiaries included the phoenix, the griffin, and the unicorn. Egyptians once believed people on the other side of the world walked upside down. Unshaped by fact, knowledge, or even by direct observation, these fantasy worlds became known as true and real in human minds at the time.

Even in later times, the relationship between nature and humanity posed a dilemma. Once it was thought that the world entered the human eye, and only through our seeing of it did it exist. There was much discussion about how a mountain could fit into the human eye. This difficulty with perspective pushed humans toward conclusions as erroneous as believing foremost in the eye of the beholder. Euclid thought the eye was the point of origin for all things. Plato believed the world emanated from the eye, while others thought that there was something given off from objects by which we perceived them. In any case, most of the theories made the natural environment smaller than it was and made the human larger. Vision was about the seer and not about the seen.

Nothing could be more different from how tribal people on all continents have seen and understood the world that surrounded the human, even in those early times. For those who remained in their own terrain for many millennia, there were—and still are—other points of view. For tribal thinkers, it is the world outside us that creates our humanity and what inhabits us. Alive to processes within and without the human, this is a more humble perception of the world, and one far more steady. Nature is the creator, not the created. The human being is not the center of the environment. This remains true. It is the reason thousands went to Standing Rock in the recent freezing winter to protect the Missouri River from the illegal Keystone pipeline of sludge that was being placed beneath the vulnerable river waters.

A geography of spirit, an individual and collective tribal soul, originates with the larger geography of nature, of the ecosystem in which we live. For tribal peoples, this has always been a constant. The animal realm, sacred waters, and the surrounding world in all its entirety is an equal to our human life. We are only part of it, and such an understanding offers us the bounty and richness of our world, one to be cared for because it is truly the being of the human.

Father Berard Haile, a priest who traveled among the Navajo in the 1930s, had his own strong Catholic belief system, but after learning only a portion of the Navajo people's ceremonies and knowledge system, Haile was in awe of their great complexity. This exists even now in the Navajo ecosystems, in all their context with the surrounding world. In the Upward Moving Way, for example, the ceremony brings in all aspects of the growth of plants: the movement upward as the roots deepen, the insects and birds that come to a particular plant. All aspects of the ceremony reveal a wide knowledge of the world of plants and all that touches them. In order for a person to heal, this outside life, the community and the world, must be taken in and "seen" by the patient as part of one working system.

Laurens van der Post, a writer, naturalist, and psychologist who grew up in Africa, wrote in his essay "The Great Uprooter" about how his son's illness was announced by a dream. In the dream, the young man stood on a beach, unable to move, watching a great tidal wave of water bearing down on him. From out of the swell of the wave, a large black elephant walked toward him. It was this dream, van der Post was certain, that announced his son's cancer, the first point of cellular change. Van der Post called the dream something that came from "the great without." Such an experience seemed to encompass, he said, all the withouts and withins a human could experience, and this kind of a large view is what we need to learn.

Nature is even now too often defined by people who are separated from the land and its inhabitants. In our time, with our lives, we usually include primarily only a majority of the developed world. Such a life is one that carries and creates the human spirit with more difficulty. Too rarely do we understand that the soul lies at all points of intersection between human consciousness and all the rest of nature. With our bodies and selves, skin is hardly a container. Our boundaries are not solid; we are permeable; therefore, even as solitary dreamers we are still rooted in the greater soul outside of us. If we are open enough, strong enough, to connect with the surrounding world, we are capable of becoming something greater than what we are merely within our own selves.

Early-twentieth-century Lakota writer Zitkala Sa (Gertrude Simmons Bonnin) wrote of the separation between humankind and the natural world as a great loss to her. In her autobiography, she said that nature was what would have helped her to survive her forced removal to Indian boarding school:

> *I was ready to curse men of small capacity for being the dwarfs their God had made them. In the process of my education I had lost all consciousness of the nature world about me. Thus, when a hidden rage took me to the small white-walled prison which I then called my room, I unknowingly turned away from my own salvation. . . .*
>
> *For the white man's papers I had given up my faith in the Great Spirit. For these same papers I had forgotten the healing in trees and brooks. . . . Like a slender tree, I had been uprooted from my mother, nature, and God.*

Zitkala Sa might have agreed with Pliny that there are dog-headed, barking men, and men with heads, not hearts, in their chests, with a mind rather than with the strength of love. She understood the loss of spirit.

Soul loss is what happens as the world around us disappears. In contemporary North American Latino communities, soul loss is called *susto*. It is a common condition in the modern world. Susto probably began when, as in many religions, the soul was banished from nature, when humanity withdrew from the world. There became only two things, extremes viewed from our point of understanding—human and nature, animate and inanimate, sentient and not.

This was the moment when the soul first began to slip away and crumble.

In the reversal of and healing from soul loss, Brazilian tribal members who tragically lost their land and place in the world and now dwell in the city often visit or at least reimagine nature in order to become whole again and have their soul returned to them. Anthropologist Michael Harner wrote about the healing methods among Indian people who were forcibly relocated to urban slums, usually from rain forests. The healing ritual most often takes place in the forest at night, as the person is returned, if only for a while, to the land he or she once knew. The people are often cured through their renewed connections, their "visions of the river forest world, including visions of animals, snakes, and plants." This connection brings back the soul that has returned to these places. Unfortunately, in our times, these places, these homes in the forests, may now only be ghosts of what they once were.

The cure for susto, soul sickness, is not found in books. It is written in the bark of a tree, in the moonlit silence of night, along the bank of a river, and in the voice of water's motion. This cure is outside of our human selves, but it becomes the thread that connects the outer world with our own.

In the 1500s, Paracelsus, considered by many to be a father of modern medicine, was greatly disliked by his contemporaries. For a while, though, he almost returned the practice of medicine to its wider place of a connected relationship by emphasizing the importance of harmony between man and nature. His view of healing was in keeping with the view that our wisest tribal elders still hold, that a human being is a small model of the world and the universe. Vast spaces stretch inside us, he thought, an inner firmament, as large as the outer world, arriving from that outer world.

What exists inside the mind is lovely sometimes, and large. Its existence is why a person can recall the mist of morning clouds on a hill, the fern forest, and the black skies of night—what the Luiseno refer to as their spirit, acknowledging how great the spirit of the world is within our own human soul. It's an enlarged and generous sense of self, life, and being, because not only is the body a creation of the world elements, but air, light, and night sky have created an inner vision, which some have called a map of the cosmos. In Lakota astronomy, the stars are the breath of the Great Spirit. It is as if the old Lakota foresaw physics and modern astronomy, the sciences that now tell us we are the transformed matter of stars, that the human body is a kind of cosmology.

The inward has, all along, been the wrong direction to seek. And yet we need the inner world, too. But we are more than that. A person seems so small, while outside them is the river, the mountain, the forest of fern and tree, the desert with its lizards, the glacial melting and freezing and the movement of all life. All this defines our own place in this world. The cure for soul loss is in the mist of morning, the grass that grew a little through the night, the first warmth of this morning's sunlight, and the human walking in a world infused with intelligence and spirit.

Part One

Eagle Feather Prayer

I thank the eagle and Old Mother for this prayer
I send to earth and sky
and the sacred waters.

I thank Old Mother and the golden eagle.
They are the ones who taught me to pray
with no words. They taught the part of me
that is unnamed by anatomy books
and so I stand,
facing you and the rest of creation
also with secret names.
I send this prayer thanking those who risk their lives
for clean, sweet water,
and once again there is the great silence
of what happened to the buffalo.

We love our horses. We love the dogs who helped us.
We love the wilderness of buffalo herds.
We are humans who love,

With no words, just part of my named self
I hold this fan from Old Mother and the eagle.
With all my strength, I send this prayer
so very silent.

One Creation

I am a warrior
wanting this world to survive
never forgotten, this earth
which gave birth to the bison, the scissortail
even the vultures of Tibet consuming the finally released
mystics, the old ones
who taught we are always a breath
away from bullets.

I am from a line of songs,
a particle of history told by the wrong people,
a country before lines of division.
In every gulley lies the power of a forest waiting.
It heard the stories elders told when they crossed
this canyon where I live. I dreamed they passed down
to the creek-bed, each human creation still present,
also loving the stones that I love, the mosses between them,
the remembered creek that runs all year.

It is hard for some to know
the world is a living being.
Some live with forgotten truth.
Others replaced truth with belief.
That's why the books of the Maya were burned
like the ones of Australia and the close North.

We can weep over such things
as lost love, as the passage away of others,
but also remember those birds, the bison,
the grief they have felt, and how the land hurts
in more chambers than one small heart
could ever hold.

Re-minding

I have friends and know many other writers who travel from one place to another to follow animal lives, or listen to biologists talk about the creations they find interesting. Some carry special camera equipment to capture a life for one brief moment in time, then study the details. But these other writers have no mustangs or burros or land to tend. They have partners or neighbors who watch over their homes while they are gone, and the means that allow for their many travels.

I once had the fortunate opportunity to follow a pod of gray whales. We followed them for a few brief years, my friend and I, writing about their journey north from birth in their Baja lagoon and back again. It was a gift. I would do it again and with the same great wonder and awe. I do wish to follow my dream someday of going to New Zealand to see the living world there and meet Maori writers. I hope to go to the Galapagos Islands. But these dreams have been exchanged for my years in one wildlife corridor. In the first range of Rocky Mountains, up and down, around a few curving canyon roads, I watch over a diverse forest and the journeys of wildlife, in addition to a single mustang and wild burro.

Driving past our small town and beyond, there is a certain curve in the dirt road that one spring day might reveal two large elk herds calmly grazing together and eating rich tall grasses. Then, the next day, twenty wild turkey may walk in their careful manner through the same great wealth of the green field. One recent full moon, a shining mountain lion walked there, its body one long golden muscle. I was with a friend. We became completely silent, motionless, watching the slow movement and the graceful animal poise before we looked at one another, our eyes showing that we had just seen the holy, the beautiful, the rare.

Remaining in this wilderness home, I have learned something of the lives here, their habits, their voices, and favored locations. Day and night, I listen. With sweet voices, does speak to the fawns outside the kitchen window. With any sense of danger, the voices of the mothers huff an exhaled breath and they are all gone. At the first hint of autumn, an elk bugles early in the morning out behind the pasture, waking me to the elk lives being lived in their own significant ways.

And I watch. Watching this year I have discovered an incredibly well-built fox den created in a hillside wall of earth along my road, its circular entrance solid as concrete. At first, I worry about whether they will catch enough food. I occasionally place eggs or some small thing across from the den before seeing the carcasses they have caught outside the opening. One day, the mother reveals her four kits as I pass through. Two are the same black color of the mother. The other two look like tortoise-shell cats, black and orange. I keep watch as they grow and soon they journey across the land, practicing fox calls and beginning the search for territories of their own.

The animal lives here have no numbers, no names. They are simply a people, nations of their own kind with lives as sacred as any of ours. I learn their ways, all different, all unlike human ways, yet all together we are one life, one breath, all part of this same shared earth. Daily, too, I hope not a single one is missing. I hope even more that on our shared part of the planet, no plant, insect, or winged creation, no walking, fur-bearing creature is in danger of being one of a lost or endangered species in this time when so many are disappearing.

A few years ago, someone above this hidden valley used a spray on trees. Bats ate the poisoned insects. No longer do bats exist in this area and I miss them. Missing now, also, are the dragonflies once here, golden eagles, and many other birds. It tells me how much power we have over all the others; we who have rights other animals do not have. And from other continents, we learn about the great number of elephant slaughters, the massacres of rhinos, lions, and now giraffes. For many of us, we hear this with a tremendous and helpless amount of grief. The numbers of lost species continue to grow daily and I am reminded that the human animal is able to take any number of lives we desire, yet not one of them can harm us without retribution: death for an entire herd, pack, or any other creature group.

I am reminded, when I hear this news. Re-minded. Exactly what so many of us need to be. We need to have changed minds, to look at new ways of thinking about our shared world. We need revised neural pathways, synapses connecting new understandings of where we stand within the whole of creation. Re-minding. Physicist David Bohm, whose own philosophical growth considered how human consciousness understands the nature of reality and our development of wholeness, has called this re-minding "the implicate order." It holds the ability of the human mind to take in the whole of the world around us.

Learning an ecosystem is like learning another language. It begins with an intimate relationship with trees, underground organisms, air currents, animal lives with their numerous pathways crossing one another on their earth journeys, all living and breathing the same air, all the same heartbeat. This relationship takes in the foods and medicines that grow from rich earth, carefully tended. It is knowledge rarely taught our children in their lessons. Many of us, even as adults, do not have the opportunity to learn our world. How rare it is when one of us learns how wolves keep elk moving to different parts of a forest territory, allowing the trees to survive and remain in healthy habitats. Another result of the wolf presence is also the continued clean and necessary water because the elk were not eating new growth, causing erosion and other events that destroyed rivers. This I learned from friend and scientist Cristina Eisenberg, who was then president of Earthwatch. A healthy forest in some locations also offers shaded waters, allowing trout and salmon to survive the heat of sunlight. Who would think that the uninterrupted presence of wolves could maintain a forest world, including waters and nesting places for bird populations with their living voices resonant in the newly deep-rooted shadows of leaves not eaten by elk and deer? How would we know these connections without many years of observation or without others available to teach us? Most tribal nations have observed their own ecosystems for many thousands of years and are able to pass on knowledge to new generations. But many nations have been removed and dislocated by the American warfare against them and by habitat change, disrupting some of their vital indigenous knowledge systems.

The place where I live is still whole in some private, untouched way. I have felt it my work to observe it or to care for it in ways that I can. I try to change nothing except when a tree breaks from heavy snow. I work at enriching the soil to its unaltered state, amending what was once deer pasture. Much labor was required after the flood of 2013, when the creek became a ten-foot river that left behind piles of debris, uprooted and broken trees, carrying them along in the rushing currents of the frightening, powerful rain and sudden snowmelt. That work is still unfinished; it is too much for a single person.

I do walk this land enough to know where one mountain lion keeps the bones of its prey, and to know where new infant forests of trees are upward rising. I remember the location of each rare wildflower I want to save from the constant hunger of the wild burro in the pasture land, wondering if I should risk moving plants to new locations. I've kept watch over the same wild blue delphinium across the creek for a few years now, keeping it safe by covering it.

At night I watch the stars and planets, entranced not by Greek astronomy but by our own ancient tribal star knowledge and cultural stories from this continent, such as the long constellation of a great horned serpent unfurled across the sky. It is often viewed with rattles and is seen in tribal nations across the entire continent. In our Southeastern sky lore, we also have a story of a canoe of star people whose happiness and singing attracted a young earth man. He fell in love with a star girl and they were married. They journey together part of the year in the sky, singing, carrying with them a smaller canoe of children born from their marriage.

These would be called the Big Dipper and Little Dipper by others. And, of course, I now see the herd of antelope the Skidee Pawnee recorded on their own complex and beautifully designed leather star chart, the sighting of which first sparked my interest in Native astronomies.

Many of our stories of the sky are similar to stories of the land. It is part of how we remember the ecosystems where we live as well as the cosmos beyond us, but few people consider, or even remember, the knowledge of stories that existed before the European entrada. Learning these is a part of the re-minding that helps us envision our world in ways that offer a chance of survival. We need the indigenous intelligence that has existed before the Europeans first stepped off ships with the broken knowledge systems that had failed the European continent.

The Maps
AFTER A VISIT TO TRIBAL ARCHEOLOGICAL SITES

Consider how the world has changed
from what it would have been
if the beaver had been left alone
to make meadows, and the river
all with its own ways of coursing through land,
changing it to another will than ours.

Consider the map if we had used seed we saved in a dry cave,
the bones of what would have been,
our great mounds shaped like eagles, turtles, water spider,
and that every 18.6 years moonlight still enters one location
in its journey, stands still and its light walks toward a great bowl
    of water,
filling it with radiance.

This Land I Live

The story of this land is ancient. The red earth, crags, and canyons were once an inland sea. I imagine the currents when this mountain basin was ocean, water swaying as the moon became full or as wind moved it, swaying. Within the water, a shining circle of fish, many lives all thinking and moving as one. Sea animals hid inside stone caves and indentations that now, so many years later, shelter canyon wrens and swallow nests, once protecting numbers of indwelling bats.

In the times that passed between all these, dinosaurs left behind their footprints and bones for humans to find and fight over. Those are on the other side of this mountain that holds me.

On a dry day with particles of dust shining in sunlight, I drove up one hill and down another, my Blackfeet friend having me stop the car several times to gather red and yellow ochre for ceremonies or to use as paint for powwow dancing. That was long ago when I lived several homes away, but even then, I looked down this valley and knew one day I would live in this home and with this land so alive, so vibrantly enchanted with songs from ancient times, and with the night animals wandering through the forest of trees or the ones crossing hillsides by day. I knew other tribes had once stayed in this place of accepted amnesty as was the rule at the hot springs not far away. The earth here is created of all their stories, ancient and new.

Even so, down below the main road, at Bear Creek, Col. Chivington planned the massacre of human beings at Sand Creek, while promising them peace and safety. This betrayal, unfortunately, is also a story of this land.

Four miles up the road, Buffalo Bill is buried, a man known only for his abuses. Not so far away from his remains is a large buffalo herd. It is a joy for me to watch them calve in the spring, then watch the light-colored calves grow and darken, but mostly it is a pleasure to witness the tenderness between mother and calf, knowing that love is an unmeasured emotion even for human beings.

Not far over the mountain, northward down a highway, the land was once a great buffalo wallow filled with large numbers of bison. Now it is the city of Denver.

I fell in love with my home a few years back when I was hiking animal trails through the forest across from here. At the time this uncared-for little place wasn't rented, so when I saw the cabin, I felt I was not trespassing. I crossed the creek and climbed up the hill, then tried to look inside. I found only one window allowing me to see a wall with wallpaper peeling like bark from a birch tree. But for me, the condition of this 1930s cabin didn't matter. The land was my gravity and eventually gravity won. All these years later, it still holds me.

This became my home twenty years after that day of window-peeking. It is land that owns me. At first, I didn't know the large number of animals that lived here and passed through, needing protection from development to the north. Nor would I have guessed I'd be years learning an environment so powerfully alive. Here are a million years of stories to tell. Some are immediate and very present, like the flattened morning grasses that reveal what slept here last night, usually a small group of doe and fawns curled together in herd dreaming. Or how the marmots across the way call out with a gentle trilling voice when they see a predator, and the three o'clock fox sings as it passes by on its daily journey with its wide tail full and beautiful. From hidden places, crows scream out and fly down to swarm their enemy, cawing loudly, alerting me to danger.

Then all becomes peacefully quiet forest and canyon once again, the singing creek passing through green mountain curves, traveling past the location where the lion keeps her bones, past the infant forest, an entire world filled with both visible and secretive lives.

Perhaps the ancestors dreamed it into existence, dreamed the future where I now live after many years of looking down into this valley with curiosity and longing, hoping I would one day live here and feel safe with the animal lives around me. I do feel that safety, living and planting above the place where water seeps out through the canyon walls, pure and clear from its secret journeys of underground miles.

I continue learning the animals, but I also want to learn the human animal. After all, we are the puzzle, the most difficult to understand or know. All the others may cohabit a field together easily: wild turkey, deer, rarely even a coyote, and the small birds at the edges. They are fine together until a human is near. Seeing us, they scatter. I am a predator known to them, when my own inner sea wants to know how we might be a part of the wilderness congress.

It is not my purpose to create a pastoral world. There are nights I hear death cries or screams of animals caught by others. I am also aware not only of the great number of species lost everywhere each day, but of the toll climate change is taking on the entire beleaguered planet. We are inundated with this pain in every book, every story on the news.

When I think of change, I consider the re-minding of ourselves and I mean that it is time to consider other kinds of intelligence and ways of being, to stretch our synapses to take in new ways of thought. As an indigenous woman, I look toward our Native knowledge systems, the times when our relationship with the earth wasn't the disjointed connection most of us have learned from our Euro-American education systems. I am one human animal who wants to take back original meanings and understandings in ways that are possible and are necessary.

Perhaps some of us make poetry, music, and art because the ancient story still dwells inside our body, as does a feeling for old ways of seeing and knowing the world. I see it in our work, our circles of Native science conversations and the popularity of our books. We also know it in some quiet moments, intimations that surface from deep in the marrow as a brief yearning. Sometimes it feels like grief, sometimes it is grace. Sometimes it is like loneliness. Sometimes a joining together with all others. In any case, it is a true and deep need, this desire to change our systems of thought and vision. In this same way, we still feel our animal kinship, our own animal life, and the primordial green and dirt-rich odor of our world connection as a reminder.

The kinship and relationship between human and nonhuman others rise from inside to seek what is relevant in this changing world. But there is more. Many of us remember this in our shared histories. We want to know what sees us when we do not know we are being watched, but only feel that watching. Our need is like the shadow attached at our feet, never to be walked away from. Instead of speaking to what is beneath that shadow, it is often easier to ignore the dialogue asked of us by earth, its language spoken within and without our own skin.

In most indigenous creation stories, humans were the last ones created. Around us are our many teachers. For now, it is enough to simply know that we do not live alone in the skin of any environment. We are part of a collective, the way marmots hibernate together in their complicated burrows beneath ground.

The World Is a House of Words

Many languages inhabit the world around us. There are times we forget our species is not of the highest intelligence, not the only ones speaking a unique language. To think in this way is a concept that David Bohm would have said is deeply entrained into our minds by what we have been taught by religious belief, education, and social training. Most humans are taught how to think through a complicated means of schooling. Unraveling this lifetime of thought is not an easy task, but our survival depends on examining this entrainment and how these mental formulations have remained with most of us through so many centuries of Western training. Yet it is possible to change entrained minds and to look beyond the teachings of a dominant system.

There are times it would be a relief to inhabit the purple-hued dark feathers of barn swallows who make pottery homes in passageways beneath roads and under the eaves of the barn, flying down to return with mud and clay in order to create their architecture for living. In the evening light, from many directions, their winged bodies fly quickly home all at once, a cloud of feathers and wings settling swiftly into place. They know their homes, know one another, care, feed, quietly speak with voices unique to them, and their languages are still being discovered. At night they curve together in the pottery dwellings created of earth, clay, and water. They are not silent in their houses, but we have not listened, nor do we consider important the knowledge they may pass from one life to the next.

Bird and animal languages are many. So are the languages of trees. The forest has exceedingly complex methods of communication still being discovered. Nonhuman languages, we have learned, are more plentiful than just the well-documented songs of water mammals who fill the oceans, more also than the enormous vocabularies of crows and ravens or the endangered prairie dogs at the edges of many towns, small burrowing animals who use numerous nouns to describe persons passing by with a language so richly developed it has a syntax and other elements common to ours. Prairie dog language has even been documented in *National Geographic* after the original studies were done.

Each nation of animals joins with all the others in an undivided terrestrial intelligence. Ours is only one part of a vast wholeness. As the brilliant thinker and writer John Hay has written, "We do not own intelligence. It is an attribute of the planet."

When I see the layers of gray fiber and saliva made into a round paper wasp nest, I marvel at its beauty and its structure but mostly I'm impressed with the way the wasps work together with one another. When the nests are abandoned and sometimes fall to the ground in winter, I save them, thinking it would be wonderful to write poetry on these thin paper-like sheets, but even better would be to know and write the story of those who created them.

My house is small and not as intricate as those of wood pulp and saliva or solid clay, or those with perfect symmetrical sections for the young. This cabin was created with stone from the land and items salvaged between wars. It is humble, but I have pride in it. It is a house I came by with words. I'd published the novel *Solar Storms*, and the home of a main character was based on this place. Because of the book, I ended up with this as my home. The seller of the cabin liked the book, bought many copies, and sold this land to me, knowing I would love and care for it. He knew I would not "scrape" the house, as they call the new approach with old homes destroyed to build larger houses on the land. I knew this home was built with love. The feeling was palpable, and so with my written words, it became my dwelling.

I call it the house of words because that was how it came to me.

The Enchanted Bedroom

Home, in the deepest sense, has many meanings. It is first thought of as an enclosure of comfort where life is lived, a dwelling place, maybe even a shell for a marine animal or a good den for wintering. But it is not just a house. It is also a part of the person who inhabits it, hopefully with comfort. As land and the terrain of memory of our lived place, it becomes a map of the heart. When I first entered this house and saw wallpaper peeling from the walls, ruined floors, and a little 1930s refrigerator with a place for two ice cube trays built into the wall, I knew every part of it would become my own.

My family gone, I needed less and this was less but outside the walls it was more. There stretched a diversity of forest, a creek, outside walls of stone canyon covered with green, gold, and black lichen. It was mosses and wildflowers, canyon and rolling hills all in one fifteen-acre parcel. The red morning sun rose between nearby mountains and there were long grasses to lie down in to watch the sky change. Many times on walks I had passed by on the upper road and looked down to this place that seemed so special and always a part of my future.

One day a realtor was putting up a for-sale sign at the top of the road. My dog and I were walking along the road, but we jumped into the truck and immediately went to the realtor's and signed the contract. Months later, I moved into the little home with the creek passing by, the forest, this wholeness all nestled together in mountain and canyon. The size of the cabin didn't matter because, for me, the outdoors was the largest part of home.

I continued to make the home like nature. I used wallpaper with ferns in the kitchen. The living room ceiling is beetle kill polished to a shine, creating a dome. Between the wood beams is still the original 1930s wallpaper of leaves. With such a ceiling, I spend much time looking up, feeling myself in the woods even while indoors, and a fireplace is made from veins of pink quartz that runs through the land. With a fire, the larger room glows on a chilly night.

Everything here says that only love has existed in this place. With everything made of this land, a person becomes part of wilderness, and I dwell in a place that lives inside my skin like the daily light and shadow, a part of the home and the land. Now here are the animals, the birds, the almost daily deer or elk outside the window eating grasses on the side rich with grain. One night a persistent bear learned to open the garage door, walk on several items I had stored, breaking most of them, and took away a bag of horse candy. I last saw it carrying the bag uphill.

This home seems as rooted as the old trees that live there. A great amount of stonework was done by one man throughout his life. He had a special love for this place. Even the long road to the house is retained by his fine stone masonry, as is the foundation of the house and a gardening area built up so the gardener wouldn't have to bend to plant or weed.

All of this together says it is a place of harmony.

I moved here still recovering from a brain injury. Besides providing harmony, this was a place of healing.

By the warmth of day, the bedroom windows were opened wide. As decoration, I had placed two painted birdhouses on the wall, one blue with a floral scene, the other white and flowered. Soon, without invitation, wasps came inside to inhabit the birdhouses. They created nests of amazing symmetry. Two decorative birdhouses, painted but not useful for birds, became the homes of wasps and we lived together easily. I opened the windows in the mornings and they went out and about their work. I closed the windows at night after they'd settled into their amazing cell-segmented homes in the birdhouses.

Not being a person afraid of wasps or bees or with insect hatred, I let them be. We kept the same daily schedule. I opened the windows in the morning. I closed them in the cooling evenings and before I went to bed. We managed to cohabit. One day I slept late and a wasp came directly over my head, closer than usual, to wake me. It buzzed loudly and I woke to open the windows and door to allow the wasps to go about their daily business. I called it the alarm wasp. I learned from this, from their way of communicating, and from their awareness and recognition of me, that they had their own form of intelligence.

For the first year, the windows of my bedroom opened inward. It was a cottage, after all, a summer cottage not meant for year-round habitation, but the wonderful thing about my beginning life in the cabin was that such great beauty surrounded me. Yet it was, and is, a small life I live here.

I brought flowers in pots to the bedroom. Blue and green dragonflies floated in from the creek. To my surprise, hummingbirds also came inside. I discovered their favorite plant was hyssop and so I planted hyssop in pretty planters throughout the room. It had a mild smell of licorice. To my amazement and delight, I watched them go from flower to flower. It was magical, as if everything spoke flowers to the lives around me.

For that summer it was that magic room, a place surrounded by forest. Though two other houses were visible, they were behind me, unseen and easy to forget their existence.

From the more visible sides of the house, there were only valley, forest, and mountains encircling me in a sense of safety, a world not safe from predators, but still within a protective circle of nature. Another word like home with its many meanings entered my mind as I sat in the room: *enchantment*, which includes within it the word *cante*, or song, a state of mind that could be transformed from the normal into the magical.

The Enchantments

All of these thoughts come to me around the word *enchantment*, a word rich and complex in meaning. This word holds great meaning, resonance, and depth. My thoughts are like the root meaning of the word. They are about a state of being but also recall the roots, *to chant* and to sing. Encant. Encantare. A story. A great poem: *canto*.

In our own tribal nation, the Chicaza, few of us hold to the oldest of ways. Reasons exist for this lack of knowledge from the past. For one thing, we are among the earliest survivors. We are descendants of the first almost colonized people when de Soto arrived on the East Coast in 1551. However, since that time, we have had many countries and religious groups bending our history, creating warfare against us, manipulating our world. Because of all this, so few ancestors had the chance of surviving unless they finally took on the ways of intruders. Colonized by many, we were still forcibly moved from our homelands to Indian Territory (Oklahoma). Through all of this, it was nearly impossible to keep our original knowledge, our first instructions from creation, our ceremonies, and our treaties with the earth and her other than human inhabitants.

My other family is Oglala Lakota. They still hold the remnants of traditional ways, but in a different sense than what I am considering here. Some have become Catholic. Some practice traditional ways. Some do both. Unlike these nations, Navajo still largely hold to the ceremonial complex called Chantways, a sacred system of myth, prayer, song, and extraordinary sand paintings, medicinal plants, and more, all connected. This elegant, intricate system is most often used for healing people, or for restoring a person to a place of emotional health. It is an old way and now many different practitioners may have only a single role in performing one long song, prayer, or other part of the ceremony, each of which is the recitation of something very ancient, complex, yet recalled for a community or for a single person.

These ceremonies are created in many ways, yet most are designed to bring a person and community into balance; *hozho* is the word meaning wholeness and harmony within their place, first within that community, then with the physical environment around them, the spiritual environment, expanding all the way out to the universe. It is an elaborate system of relationships, with a mere human standing in place within the greater entirety.

From the first creators, from mythic creation and the world's early inhabitants, and with the inclusion of sacred lands, animals, and plants of the mountain-bounded world, the remembered words and songs carry harmony to a restored world.

This re-creation takes place through language and image, songs and prayers, through the speaking of a people's original knowledge. It is akin to the power of enchantment, an intelligent word that holds all stories spoken. It holds the spirit close in a state of awe and wonder. This realm dwells in the heart of each small human. It lives at our soul depths. But first we learn to become conscious of the smallness of our human self and the greatness of the world around us. This consciousness appears in a moment caught within our full beauty.

One spring, many years ago, I went to the deer dance of the Yaqui in Arizona. This dance is a ceremony passed down from ancient and unmeasured time. In daylight was the singing and much more that, as an outsider, I would not know. Dancing took place in the church courtyard, with women dressed in black and mourning. Everywhere in the desert realm were evergreen sprigs. Clowns appeared. The day passed with much activity and, even as an observer, I felt its profundity. I didn't want to leave. I didn't want to walk away from something so clearly meaningful, and so remained late. Late into the night, one man danced tirelessly and without end, wearing white buckskin and the head of a deer above his human head, with flowers and evergreen in his antlers. Firelight, or moonlight, shone on his skin. Singing took place as he danced himself out of one world and into another, a state of what The People call true enchantment. Later I read that it was a song cycle; it begins in the enchanted mountain forest with the story of a young deer or fawn coming out of the mountain evergreen trees with spring flowers in its antlers, as it is written in one of many books:

Flower-covered fawn went out,
enchanted, from each enchanted flower.
Wilderness world,
he went out.
Flower-covered fawn went out,
enchanted from each enchanted flower
wilderness world,
he went out.

This is only one version of the beginning, and it's important for us to note that the mountains are still the center of the Yaqui world, even though the people were pushed by the Spanish into the desert. Again, the realm of cantos, stories, songs, and dance returns a people to the past, and the past to the present. To the people a sense of wholeness begins with that first hypnotic passage and moves to some parts of life before invasion, from inside the first world.

Reading the songs of different deer dance singers, all speak of the world of story, and how song and dance are a part of enchantment, bringing the human into a more-than-human realm, a consciousness too rarely beholding the world. *Beholding* is the correct word because this dance and the days around it derive from seeing the world with deep human awe.

From the roots of enchantment, something of our lives in their broken parts come together to make for wholeness. Wholeness. Completeness. It begins with something as ancient as that memory of the young deer coming from the forest with spring flowers entangled in its antlers.

For Native people, harmony and wholeness are of importance in our lives. Words and songs have been a key to open that harmony. In Christianity, even in the Creation story of the Bible, the world was created with words of God saying *Let there be*. And there was. The word *God*, itself, according to the origin of its meaning is a word that means to call out, to invoke, or to address. Perhaps we have not just words or an invocation, but more than that. For many nations, wind enters our lives with our first breath at birth and it carries us through life. It even creates who we become. At death our breathing returns to the wind. Air, spoken words, wind, all alive. This is a small planet. We breathe what the elk breathes, or that spring deer coming from the evergreens. Our breath crosses continents. Close in, I breathe the forest plants around me. It is the same breath of horse, deer, mountain lion, bear, even the hiss of rattlesnake.

Those who came to this place long ago traveled long distances. Tribal seekers and hunters dwelt here in these rocks. Some came to pray and pay respect to these lands. I think of their voices at night when I'm outside listening to the poorwill and horned owl and when I hear plants move in the breeze, or by daylight when a blooming tree is alive with the hum of bees taking in the pollen. I listen and sometimes I sing my own songs back to what I hear around me.

Considering the world of plants as a part of all this, a botanist friend reminds me that not only do the plants heal, but a song goes with each plant that heals.

Eduardo, the Peruvian healer, called his own form of healing "the enchantments." In his litany of healing or of finding a lost item, he recites not only the names of mountains, place names, but those of all lives around them: Red Mountain, White Mountain, Red Wolf, White Dog. He goes calling, with the beautiful flowering gardens, the sun and moon and the herbs, he goes calling, naming all this "the keeping of accounts."

Eduardo, when he was alive, said, "Let us go calling and accounting for this world." These are my accounts, my stories and songs, small events in a large world.

Part Two

Elk Dog
THE HORSE

Standing tonight in a small wind with two horses, the chill of early Colorado autumn is fresh in the air. The woody scent of blowing dry leaves joins with the odor of pine and sweetness of juniper. Behind me, in the old dead tree called a "snag," is the little pygmy owl. He lives inside a hole first created by woodpeckers seeking insects. Over time, the hole has grown larger, darker.

The horses listen to the wind. Night sky holds close the depths of the universe and as one constellation slowly moves toward the west another rises from the east. On my mind are the times when our valued indigenous astronomers watched star maps carefully.

For our Southeastern nations, long before the known Greek constellations, a great hand reached the western edge of earth to help the souls of the dead rise up to journey through the spiral road of the Milky Way where spirits joined others in the afterlife.

It seems that for many of the first people familiar with their ecosystems, lives on earth also took shape in the sky. These were known for millennia before Pegasus, yet Ptolemy recorded forty-eight horse constellations. But the horse as we know it now didn't return to this land until later in our histories.

The horse is the only European animal that entered tribal my-thologies and stories of our First Peoples. Considered sacred an-imals, the Aztecs placed red cloth on the ground for the horse to walk upon. Now these animals are found in stories and songs throughout North America. This section of a Navajo Chantway, speaks of the reverence held for horses:

His fetlock is like a fine eagle plume.
His legs are like quick lightning.
My horse's body is like an eagle-plumed arrow.
My horse has a tail like a trailing black cloud.
I put flexible goods on my horse's back.
The little Holy Wind blows through his hair.
His mane is made of short rainbows.
My horse's ears are made of round corn.
My horse's eyes are made of big stars.
My horse's head is made of mixed waters.
From the holy waters, he never knows thirst.
My horse's teeth are made of white shell.
The long rainbow is in his mouth for a bridle,
And with it I guide him.
When my horse neighs, different colored horses follow.

For Chicaza people, the horse was first called Elk Dog and Wolf Elk. Everywhere, they had similar names. Most think of Indian horses first on the Northern Plains or with the Nez Perce, but they entered our southern lands in the mid-1500s. We bred short Spanish Barbs long before horses reached those other regions of the country. Our own beloved breed became a major part of our trade system. It is said that their necks were not long and that sometimes they bent a leg to graze the rich grasses. Fast runners, muscular workers, some are believed to have remained from De Soto's stay with the Chicaza in 1551 near the once-wide

Tombigbee River where we lived when they arrived, dressed in armor, probably overheated, hungry, and with a history of horrific violence we knew because news traveled quickly from nation to nation. There were no secrets.

Unknown to most Indian horse people, horses of the Southeast were once just called "Chickasaws," as I was told by Elder Tom Phillips in one of our long conversations. I find no other documentation of this, but I do find it certain that they would have been in great demand, and these horses were soon moved across land, then up and down the Mississippi River on flatboats. We had extensive trade networks with other nations far away. We all lived by such trade and friendships, not by war, as is often said by historians.

One of these Spanish Barb horses came to me in a roundabout way through an accident I had with another horse I thought I might buy. Because of numerous injuries, including fractures in the pelvis and a serious brain injury, I woke in a brain and spinal cord hospital. I have no memory of the accident. I was found broken and bleeding on a dirt road near my home. Hospitalized, I spoke words and stories I no longer recall.

Trying to walk again, to learn skills, I watched the site of Colorado Horse Rescue. I'd been on their waiting list for at least two years, ever since purchasing the small cabin with fifteen acres. While still in the hospital, I fell in love with a large black tender-looking horse named Alf without realizing his great size. I sent him cards and sweetgrass. Clearly the barn keeper and workers realized I wasn't in my right mind when mail arrived from a hospital, and it was from a woman looking at a horse so large a special wagon had to be built to trailer him when he was finally adopted by a family and taken to his new home where he was loved by all.

But I was recovering. Such an interesting word, a body healing being akin to the way certain plants take over the life of broken earth. Still, it was not the condition in which I wanted to find myself after having nearly been killed by a horse. I wanted to heal a brain that now had two gray spots where synapses were broken, where memories once lived, including the memory of the accident, which was gone. Now and then I have a glimpse of the crazy horse racing out of control to the top of a hill and jumping. I can't know if the saddle slipped. I tried to put together the injuries, the fractures in the pelvis, injuries to the right foot, injured neck, the head that must have hit earth more than once but with the worst injury to the left-brain region, causing the brain to hit the front right of the skull bone, twisting that soft organ in the center and partially dividing two hemispheres. Two brains. Like a dolphin, I thought more than once. Maybe instead of needing the sleep I rarely had, I now had two minds. But the man who later tested me said I would never be able to work at anything again, although I did recover, at least in part.

Returning home, I never remembered I couldn't walk, and I continued to fall. But healing takes place, even in the hardness of bones. One day, to the horror of my family, I received a phone call from the horse rescue. They thought they had a horse for me. Still far from healed, I nevertheless went right away with my crutches—not the walker—to look at the horses. I still wanted to fulfill my dream and find a horse. By then it must have been spring. Wildflowers grew near my home, but out east at the horse rescue, everything was dry with wind occasionally blowing up dust devils. Still, I heard a meadowlark. Looking around were many other people looking at the rescued horses, which were in various kinds of shape: hungry, injured, elderly.

The barn manager wore a dirty Carhartt jumpsuit and was herself dirty with a thin, tanned face. She was outside, dusty, and leaning against the entrance, smoking a cigarette as she sized up my inexperience and the shape I was in. I felt childlike and ignorant in comparison. I was now a person with poor memory and crutches, but there I was, looking at horses. Her eyes spoke her thoughts about my stupidity, as if we were two different species.

An expansive, cheerful volunteer walked me about, but stopped more than once at a round pen containing a dark-faced pitiful horse. Finally, she mentioned how the horse looked at me more than once and seemed to be claiming me as hers. I think she knew I'd believe her, or perhaps this was the horse they planned for me all along, the safest, the hungry and overly thin, hooves filled with blood, body scarred and branded. I went back and looked again. Nearby someone patted a horse and dust flew out of the fur. Little did I know that dust was a word that later defined much of my life.

Soon, again with the sound of a meadowlark on the dry Colorado prairie, I took this horse for the required walk, not an easy task with crutches. One crutch fell. The horse stopped, looked at the crutch, looked at me, and waited, as if realizing that I was also not whole. I, too, was scarred in some way.

This became my horse. Her name was Kelly.

Papers needed to be filled out. Questions about caretaking a horse needed answering. As the woman asked the questions, she answered them herself, saying, Right, two flakes of hay at a feeding, and, Yes, she will need senior feed supplement. I signed the papers she pushed toward me. Outside I saw another woman, much older than myself, being pulled about by a large stallion. I watched them, thinking she'd never handle such a horse, but the small, fragile, gray-haired woman said to the manager, "I'll take this one." Soon, at another desk, she also signed papers, honestly answering questions.

I knew none of the information on feed, so I kept a copy of the instructions, paid the fee, and bought a horse with severe malnutrition, blood in her hooves, and her head hanging low, as if even she believed she might not survive. She had scars, and not from a poor saddle.

It seemed only minutes before a tiny woman driving a large truck with a trailer came dusting through the gate and then straight toward us. She, Lori, loaded my new Kelly into the trailer and drove to her farm in Arvada, where other pitiful, rescued horses lived in fenced pens with various kinds of shelter.

As Lori drove, Kelly looked back from the trailer the entire time to be certain I was following, that I was her new human, that she had a home. My heart broke at the same time I felt happy and smiled to reassure her. She was not a pretty horse, but once unloaded, Lori said, "Isn't she beautiful? She's such an Arabian." Lori saw Kelly's future.

And she truly was. She became increasingly beautiful with an adequate diet and care. Her face lost its darkness. Lori had seen it the moment we trailered her. I saw only a pitiful horse needing help, one a crazy British woman said had taken several looks and claimed me! I was still vulnerable. It took little to con me in this world now, but I set about learning the practical art of horse care and beginning to understand our manner of communicating with one another, human and horse.

It seems to have all taken place in a very short time. Even injured as I was, this horse adoption now seems like a dream. So did my injuries at the time. Even disabled I managed to go to my pre-arranged journey to the gray whale birthing lagoon at San Ignacio against my brother's insistent wishes and forceful demands that I was not capable. After all, I was still on crutches. To him, I was not thinking "right." Perhaps I wasn't, but I was as insistent as he was. They were whales, after all, and it was a long-planned, fortunate journey. Finally, convinced he couldn't sway me, he decided to go along to keep me safe. After all, he'd been the good brother who remained by the couch where I slept each night, because I couldn't remember I had a fractured pelvis and kept falling. As a part-time wildlife photographer, while there, he took several beautiful photos. To his surprise, his picture of young whales eating eelgrass saved the lagoon from becoming a deadly salt factory planned by Mitsubishi. He was congratulated. His work was loved. I was proud of him. He, too, has a heart for animals.

During the next months, I continued to give talks and readings, one on the same whales for the Humane Society. Other talks I've never recalled even though I was able to remember so much of my life before the accident.

I continued to visit the horse at Lori's and we became friends as I had a fence built on part of the land I'd bought. I wanted to bring Kelly home. Not wanting to interfere with the wildlife corridor, there were only specific areas I used for horse pasture. I still had an insistence; I bought the land to save it from development and I planned to leave it safe for the future. But now I was also the keeper of a horse I knew little about, though to my surprise this mare had papers and the brand inspector agreed that they were correct. So why was she neglected and abused? What did her previous owners, however many there were, have on their minds? Cruelty to animals touched my life. Even as a child, I had fought it in every way possible.

Lori and I were close friends. She was my teacher of care, of horses and other animals, the little goats and lambs she loved. I went to the farm daily while still writing. The dog found great joy there. Kelly was gentle. Each day, I led her to green grass for a special treat while my dog, part greyhound, ran through fields with joy, never bothering the horses. He was a favorite to everyone as I cared for Kelly.

A mustang named Misty was at the same farm. Her indifferent owners hadn't paid her board and she had only a small canvas for protection. To them, she was "ugly," merely a body they believed would give birth to a black foal, having bred her with the perfect black stallion.

My friend Brenda first noticed her and soon Misty began to receive my attention, but so did many of the other rescued horses there. One adopted horse was blind. One was bought off a slaughter line and didn't have enough teeth to eat, but was cared for and loved by a woman who purchased magnetic blankets and other unique things for her. Worried about a toothless horse, I stopped at a juice bar one day and asked if I could have the pulp left over from their juicing. Glad to not waste it and happy it went to good use, they gave it to me. To the compassionate owner's delight, the grass and carrot pulp began to fatten her girl. Soon she, too, was seeking pulp and finding other ways to feed the toothless equine. We horse women became a community.

And so, concerned about the pregnant mare, after Kelly's daily walk, I also walked Misty, the gray mustang, to fresh grasses. She grew round and heavy. One later day I saw the infant moving inside her. Shortly after, walking Kelly, she stopped, one front leg bent to the ground. I knew she'd ripened and was ready to give birth. I told Lori. She checked her, agreeing. At home I packed up all I needed to stay the night, maybe longer, and the dog and I returned. Lori and I put down straw in a shelter for the birth, and also in one corner for ourselves to witness this moment. We sat and waited, silent.

Eventually we saw something that might have been a first sign of birth. Waters may have flowed. I don't recall. But unlike the way a foal is born with front feet first swimming out, Lori saw something else. A visiting vet earlier thought things were going well. But Lori went over to look, then returned and said she'd never seen anything like it before but it looked like an ear. She couldn't be sure. Not knowing enough about the dangers of foaling. I thought the infant was listening to the world it was entering, but Misty, on that night when things went wrong, suffered pain beyond pain. Watching her made me weep. I begged any gods for mercy.

On the night of her terrible pain, Misty put her head in the water tank and shook it, as if trying to drown. Lori had seen this only once before, and it was with a dying horse. The short mustang fell to earth and rose again, then fell, finally stopped by pain, and not getting up. The infant was moving inside but it was terrible to see that the foal was only creating more pain. Misty moaned. The earlier visit with the vet had seemed to go well, but on the second trip, he reached inside, then said the foal was large and before long he said it had died of a broken neck. I always believed, I knew, he understood it would have kicked her to death from inside and with that reach inside her, he broke the neck of the foal. It quit moving. But no one else would swear by it. It was so sudden. In any case, she had to get up, and she couldn't. She had to go to the hospital. Soon the others began to whip her in order to force her to her feet and into the trailer. Told to get a whip, I knew I couldn't whip her. They yelled at me to hurry or she would die. Unwillingly, I ran, then returned with a whip, but I knew I couldn't inflict more pain on the poor suffering mare. Already the whipping was without results, but they wanted more. As I returned, whip in hand, I stood before the mare who wasn't mine, and with all my human might, my inner strength, with heart and all the energy I could summon and pull together of myself, I lifted my arms before her. I raised my arms. With some understanding between us, she rose to her feet. She, who had held her head beneath water in her pain and lay writhing, pushed herself up on bent legs from hard earth, stood still a moment, then walked straight into the trailer. To my great relief and gratitude, she understood. She trusted me. In that moment, we were spirit to spirit, heart to heart. Perhaps she knew I was no foreigner to physical pain, that I walked only because I had medication, ill long years even before the injuries from a horse I only remembered as a crazy one who left me bleeding and unconscious on the road.

I followed the horse trailer to the hospital. When we arrived, she was placed standing in a squeeze pen and given an epidural. The relief she had was tangible. She exhaled, then breathed. I touched her face. I rubbed her neck. I scratched her mane, then smoothed my hand over her eyes, closing them gently. Her eyes had already seen too much of this human world, a violent roundup from the wild, pain, no love, more pain with this failed birth, and she was young, four at the most. From that moment, knowing her great suffering, her momentary relief, I felt a closeness to her. The veterinarian removed the infant, having to cut the beautiful black foal. It lay on the cement floor with a broken neck and body, wet, shining, bleeding, all in a shape that said, I am here. Love me. I am curled up as if asleep. I am ready to exist.

After the surgery, the vet wanted payment. That was nothing we'd even considered at the time. It was extremely expensive after two visits, trailering, medicine, surgery, and everything that would follow to keep her from infection or other problems. We all looked at one another. He said he would have to put her down. It crossed through my mind that the surgery was done, why kill her now, but sometimes it is not always about healing. I asked if he took credit cards. So with plastic, I bought the mustang who has lived with me now for over twenty-two years, always right outside my window.

I didn't know horses cried, but on the way back, and for days after, Misty wept. Tears fell from her eyes. I knew she cried from grief. She looked back each time she dropped manure, as if it might be the foal. She still awaited its birth, until finally she realized she had no movement inside, and no small life would ever come from her. Her nipples dripped milk. The vet said she had a broken pelvis from the roundup in addition to the other problems. Like me, only I was still trying to walk easily and recover from fractures in my pelvis.

U.S. is still visible on Misty's body. United States. It is the brand that says she comes from this land and belongs to "America." I thought how that was so like us with our tribal enrollment numbers. My grandparents are named and numbered on the Dawes Act Rolls. Our own names, too, have numbers behind them on the Chickasaw rolls. The United States identifies and claims those of us from this earth, named, registered, branded. The mustang had been branded just below the mane. Daily it reminds me that she is a part of wilderness, the survivor of old history. Yet her dark and seeing eyes say not only that she loves but that she will never be owned. As a friend said, "Wild horses know who they are." They do. She does. She always has. It is spoken by her manner. Her eyes see through the wood of barns when someone passes by on the other side. She sees past barriers into the far distances as if longing for her old freedom. She knows if anything in the area moves or makes a sound.

Kelly now had a needed companion. Soon they came to live here in our small town. It had been sudden to have one horse. Now I had two. As the fences was still being built, the little place repaired, the horses went to live across the main street of our town the next mountain over with its large pasture, a mountain meadow, river, trees, and grasses. It was a healthy mountain hillside. It had riding trails. In the beginning, Misty was placed in a solitary pen until we saw how she would interact with the others. Kelly, who was easy in the herd, remained near her most of the time. After a week or more of kicking, Misty was freed and soon became the head mare of the herd. She was young, but she came from the wild and knew how to survive, to smell the location of water, even where the water table was close enough to the surface to provide the best grass. She listened for predators or trespassers and knew how to attack. They'd have no chance to harm the others. These are important skills in predator country. She was the wisdom horse it was said, not bred or educated to purposes having to do with human needs, desires, or appearances. One who wouldn't need shoes as her feet were strong, perfect.

With Misty, I often think that somewhere in the past my ancestors knew hers. We had a deep connection. We knew one another. Mystery was at work with us, a deep kinship.

With Kelly, our relationship was one of mutual respect, great love, and affection. We had gratitude for one another. She was gracious and loving. With each horse, our way of being together was different.

Little time passed before the large acreage was sold to a developer. This was difficult for many of us who kept our horses there. We loved the land and trees. The horses were bonded and we boarders had also bonded with one another, even with each other's horses. We rode together. I didn't ride Kelly, still worried about her strength, but one day I rode Misty with a few others along a trail and Misty laid down while I was on her. I got off right away. One of the other riders laughed. "That's the evil pony routine. Next time stay on so when she gets up you'll still be in place."

We all would miss this land that didn't need to be sold. The woman was wealthy already. But soon I walked my two horses across the main street to my little home. By then the fencing was finished and I was moved into the now hundred-year-old cabin.

The two horses became inseparable over the years. Nothing was as perfect for them as the large pasture across the way and the larger herd. Over here, mountains and crags and thicker forests shade the grasses of an arid world and the field grasses are thin and quickly consumed. Yet it is a timeless place with a history all its own and the voice of a creek in all seasons. Also, the song of the marmots, the fox that crossed the hills daily at three o'clock, a breeze moving grasses and leaves. Here is not a place of words or human intrusion, but one of listening, an ancient world where fish once swam an inland sea and stone was pushed sideways in glacial layers of red and burgundy. Dinosaur prints are on the other side of this mountain, attracting tourists and scholars.

As for the horses outside my windows that are always open when warm enough, we speak to one another in evening soft voices. Mornings they are all beautiful mane and running hoof. They know when it is time to eat.

In the season when animals change color, when rabbits turn darker, I was brushing Misty and my friend said it looked like snow, but her fur was all around us. Afterward, while she ate hay, I bent and picked up the fur by the handful and put it into a bag. She'd been white except for the few gray and black Appaloosa spots. Now she was becoming dark. Sometimes she is black, sometimes white. All her different colors are found in bird's nests in this region. She changes color several times a year, either a wild trait or a genetic one belonging to her, a blue-roan identified by long red belly hairs the color of water willows in the spring.

She still is noble and self-knowing. With each of them, I would never know what was under their own intelligent surface, but they had layers of other intelligence and long memories, still displaying fear at times, their histories with past owners. As human beings do not forget their own past traumas or loves, neither do horses.

But the radical awareness, the intelligence of horses, is in their knowledge of human intention, their intuition, and in the personal stories that offer insight into their behaviors. They know my intent before I step out the door. If it has to do with something they do not like, they have already planned how to make my job impossible.

Standing out at night or in early mornings with the two mares, I think often of the ancient human interest in horses, like Ptolemy seeing at least forty-eight in his star maps or the Chauvet Cave with its numerous horse paintings, drawings, and the often mentioned large carved found bone that is still considered a masterpiece of art, perfectly cut and finely etched into the head and neck of a horse. It was so finely done, it is remarked on as one of the great historical pieces of art for its realism and fine muscular detail. These visions in the world of Chauvet were hidden for many years by the cave's collapsed entrance.

The horses at Lascaux Cave run across stone walls, fully muscled and detailed, while in the same place, human animals are often only stick figures. For once, we are small in a world powerful with other life-forms. It is clear that horses have been worshipped and adored and depicted as more real, more important than the women and men who painted them in the caves where long-hidden magnificent creatures still run through the darkness, mystical, superior, fully formed, and alive.

Several years ago, a new light in the sky was considered a new planet, farther from the sun than earth. In truth, its bright presence may still be an unknown. I watch for it. Tonight, standing out with horses, I also contemplate and wish to learn this earth, from rich soil, diatoms, strands of tree fungus, and microorganisms all communicating, to how one drop of ocean water contains more life than a large city.

One mare, derived from the word *ocean*, is nuzzling me, her own inner world still unknown to mine. With the unique dignity of other lives, I understand how they may have been the original gods while we were merely stick figures, known to the others.

We were finally settled here at the cabin when Lori, my friend from the farm, came to visit. It was the last time we saw one another. Her cancer had progressed. It was overcoming her quickly and seeing her just before death, she was glowing, as if the reach of death was a place in the light. She was beautiful, bald, and shining. She was happy to see Kelly in her place and healthy. Lori's husband, Ted, carried her out to the pasture to watch the horses in spring when everything, even the horses, seemed fully blooming as they ran across the land to Lori and Ted, thrilled to meet their old friends once more.

The couple stayed for coffee and when they left, I knew it was the end and I wept. I wouldn't see Lori again. He had carried her because she was weightless. Soon she was gone.

The day of the funeral, the friend who drove me to the funeral home didn't want to go to "some Christian thing," as she believed it would be. Unable to talk me out of going, she left me there, then later relented and came inside to sit beside me. I took her hand.

It was the best sending-off of one beautiful human being. All of our pictures and all the horses they'd boarded or known were on the many shelves surrounding the room. Friends spoke of her and all her kindness. It was a room filled with people, all kinds, but primarily cowboys and horsewomen, even those who'd bought magnetic blankets for horses they loved. Most touching was the music as we left, "Happy Trails to You."

How I've missed Lori and thought so often of our times together, the time I called the vet for her little goat. The vet told me the market price of a goat compared to a vet visit on a Saturday. Lori, listening in, said, "But I love her." There were too many animals, and not enough income, always too many bills and no one could guess the price of feed, so I paid the vet to visit the goat who'd only overeaten new grass. Anything was worth the compassion of this small woman, the little cowgirl who'd grown up with orange crates for tables, tree stumps for chairs, a poverty that grew a woman who loved deeply, had always wanted most a glass cabinet to show off her special items without all the dust of horse life. I remember her stories and history. Once, walking at night to search for a herd, she lit a match to check her location only to discover she was surrounded by a silent pack of wolves. The light from her matches sent them away, and she believed it kept her safe.

In the Chicaza past, when we called horses Elk Dog, indigenous people understood it is not only with our eyes or minds that we see this world, but also with our hearts and flesh. We see it with the stories that created us; without these, we'd have no real sense of ourselves or our context. Stories carry us from the ancient past to the future. A more recent one has remained with me as part of my existence. The words give me hope for the future in this time when so many feel hopeless, when talk of the Anthropocene surrounds and impedes every gathering. In spite of these discussions, rarely do I see those speakers creating significant work, saving strangers or elders, or seeing animals in their own full being. Something deep within says we can work together and find unity in some way, find a better future instead of only the division around us.

A friend worked in the tribal department of fish and game. He was essential in returning buffalo to his people who had long lived as their relatives on the Great Plains and grasslands. He told about returning buffalo after the dreary time of their deaths and terrible absence, killed by cruel shooters who wanted to bring an end to the Northern Plains people, and had no respect for any lives already on this continent.

When he and others returned the bison, the weight of their hooves brought water back to the surface. Soon the original ecosystem that had been forgotten by all but a few elders once again had streams and creeks that had been missing for numerous years. The weight and heft of the great hooves brought back water that, in places, ran across the land, feeding great tall grasses beneath the surface, now tall in their season, gold and carrying seed in winter. All this had ceased to exist without the buffalo. Now the grasses rippled like ocean waves in the wind. Seeds attracted insects. Wildflowers returned. Insects drew birds long gone from the region. Soon, even berries came back. Reptiles and other forms of life, as if from inner earth, made holes in the ground, creating, as prairie dogs do, a rich and living soil.

One herd, one collective mind, renewed the world.

Years later, it was decided to bring in a herd of wild horses. When the horses were released to the prairies and wild grasses, they ran with great pent-up energy across the land, free, and thundering across earth, their joy so enchanting that the buffalo stood quietly at the top of a hill watching the beautiful, muscular horses.

Anyone who sees a herd of equine life and power run across land knows the awe and sheer power of the horses, their thunder rising up from such delicate legs and hooves. With that return of the buffalo, all of this began with one person's hope and vision. Those two qualities are our future. The vision of imagination and of restoring the earth, the hope of maintaining the lives of all animals, all waters, and the health of soil.

As for the horses, a Mandan leader said, "My god is the horse." I remember these words and the losses of their people, their desperate need for horses. His words remain true.

Each morning, I watch the mustang run to the far end of the pasture and back. She is a strong and forceful wind, a river of water running down from the mountain. Her hooves pound earth. She could easily be recognized in the Buddhist perspective as elemental living motion.

A silent language passes between us as we stand together in stillness, my hand on her, her head turned back to look at me, or when we move together, riding as one being. It is a relationship of mutual spirit, a connection that has no name but I call it love. Still, love is only part of it. Between us is also the beauty of compassion, a quality that enlarges a human being. It draws us together with the holy, the sacred, the many kinds of spirits that exist in our world and sky, like the ones that appeared when the buffalo herd went home after the years of having been remembered as only bones and hide when their lives and ways could have offered, even taught, something vital to the newcomers in this land if only they'd listened, if only they had felt.

In our human place, we are only one of earth's beings, surrounded by other intelligences we seek to understand.

Indian Territory

We moved to my homeland of rural Oklahoma, where I worked for my tribal nation for six years. I moved to a home that offered freedom for Kelly to walk and eat grass anywhere. Often, she stood at the window and watched me type and work at the desk. After my many years of loving and caring for her as she grew healthy, she now wanted to keep track of me.

Kelly had turned gray in the face. She had special supplements for arthritis. By then she was thirty or older, but still running toward me when I drove home from work. And still running with Misty, her wild and loved sister. The inseparables.

Kelly, my first horse love, had grown old. One day she was unable to get up. It was her time, I knew, with a fracture of my heart. That day we waited four hours for a vet to come from Texas because no facilities were in the area, no vet, no help of any kind. It was a small town grown from and still holding to the corruption and theft that remained from the time when land was stolen from Indian people in the earlier part of the century.

It was a hot day. Waves of heat rose from the cracked, dying earth. I sat in a folding chair or on the earth with Kelly's head on my lap, holding a red umbrella over her in the strong heat, wishing she might be saved. I sang old horse songs, ours. I wiped her face with a cool damp cloth. When the vet arrived four hours later, what I suspected was true: he couldn't save her. We managed to walk her to where I would bury her between two large trees. Once again, she fell to the cracked, dry red Oklahoma earth. In that place, as she looked into my own loving eyes, he put her down with a needle, quietly, quickly, so easily. Then he left as I tried to figure out what to do with the great horse body.

Misty came and remained, seeing that her sister no longer breathed. She walked around her, her black face close to her companion of many years. She stood with her at holy attention. I wrapped Kelly as well as possible in an Indian blanket. I wanted a ceremony, a quiet burial. I'd brought tobacco, Apache sage, and other items to bury with her. But I realized there was no way to bury her with grace when the backhoe came, all noise and an operator who needed to get back to his job. Once the hole was dug, there was the problem of how to lower her body. It did not go well and most of the strength came from me. My friend had the use of just one arm and the backhoe driver wasn't motivated. It not only hurt my body to help her down the darkness of the earth womb. It hurt my heart to see how she fell, not gently as I wanted, but landing with her neck bent.

I planted the mound above her with bulbs and native flowers on this land once a Choctaw allotment before it came down to me. It was purchased after years from those who'd stolen it. I planted the land. It was indigenous earth, ours after the long trail where so many of us died. I knew the name of the first Choctaw man here and my heart breaks at how the lands were lost. My own family lost home, along with most other Chickasaws during those days of theft by the government, settlers, squatters, thieves with lawyers, lawyer thieves, and then The Dawes Act, which was created by the government to lessen our lands.

I planted the mound over Kelly thinking all the earth here was a human graveyard from the time we arrived in this place, where our removed tribes had land belonging to other tribes, all of us forced to live like white people in order to survive, especially after the fear from Wounded Knee, when my grandparents were young. I planted the red earth over my Kelly in a place surrounded by pitiful strays, dog fighters, pit bull breeders, the KKK, and Christians not what they professed. We all soon left Oklahoma.

Before going to my homeland, in Southern Oklahoma, I'd learned much about working with horses. With Kelly, I learned that most important was the way they know my intentions no matter how I tried to hide them. That is one cognitive skill most humans lack. With Kelly and Misty, I'd also learned never to pull a horse around with reins, kick them, or any of those cues seen in movies as ways to get a horse to obey, when all a rider need do is look at where they wish to go. Our intent is felt through the slightest movement of the human body, down the spine to the horse mind. The horse will turn to follow the eyes. I now see those other ways as abuse. As a Hopi man my father knew had said, "No metal in the mouth or on the feet." Since then, I've seen the horseshoes made of woven fibers, and the Plains horse thieves of long ago used only a rope between the teeth and carried with them an empty bag to be filled with grass as their saddle.

As for the metal, I recall reading that when Chickasaw leaders came to Indian Territory to search for the appropriate lands to purchase, Southern Plains tribesmen were friendly until seeing the horseshoes, which they associated with white enemies. Problems then ensued. After this, unknown to us, our first choice of land belonged to Mexico, as did much of the U.S. then.

My father's stories of earlier times were many. Our family experience with horses was eloquent and shared on our nights outside together telling stories. The historical materials he shared remain with me the most. He was born in 1913 and the struggles between tribal nations and the United States were not yet over. As a young boy, he recalled Indians coming from other nations in the dark of night to his father. Some, he said, were "real Indians, not like us. They wore loincloths and everything." Hiding from the cavalry, refreshing horses, sleeping, eating, and talking about what was happening with their nations, my grandfather helped his friends from afar, even though as people who came over the Trail of Tears, we seemed much like the colonizers to some. My father, who heard only Chickasaw at home, still considered the others more real than himself. This is heartbreaking to me. It is the identity crisis of so many descendants of the Trail of Tears.

My father told of mule races in those days, then later, the army mule train that people loved to see on exhibit. But never did I hear about wild burros or donkeys, although one Puerto Rican writer, Juan Ramón Jiménez, who in the past wrote a book about a donkey, received the Nobel Prize in literature, and paintings and petroglyphs of donkeys exist in early Egyptian art. They are usually bearing loads, which is too bad for an animal of exceptional intelligence. As one unremembered person said, Donkeys might carry the weight of gold, but they eat only hay and straw.

Later I adopted one of these straw-eating burros as a companion for Misty.

Raindancer, the wild burro, was one of many burros at the Bureau of Land Management facility.

In Pauls Valley, the horses were large, wild, and crowded together. This made them appear too powerful for me. They had no chance to coalesce into a herd, more of them constantly being added. It was troublesome and painful to watch. And, so, the companion for Misty turned out to be a wild and very young burro. The burros also were plentiful, hundreds of them, all afraid, stressed, none trained or having been with humans.

I had two friends with me. They helped pick Rainy. She was the dark one, the one who seemed most needy, not fitting in with the golden beauties, all with dark crosses on their backs said to be the result, or the gift, from the burro carrying Mary and Jesus. Raindancer, too, is marked with a cross, only it is black against her darkness and nearly invisible.

Named for the white spots beneath her eyes, the lines of white down her face, for her dancing legs, likely to dance away from me too easily; the name, Raindancer, fits perfectly. I have learned many things from equines. Being with them is an experience that keeps me active and alive, physically busy and in shape. But they learn more about us. They know what I know. My hope is that, mistreated, hungry, and damaged, they might learn that human beings have compassion, patience, and love, that many of us are capable of being kind.

I continue to call Rainy small, although she is now as tall as Misty. I knew nothing about a burro, their great intelligence, their amazing abilities and beauty, the prehensile lip that can reach a long distance to gather food, or their constant need for food and extra fiber. After a few years, I am still learning her ways as she learns mine, that when I have a plastic bag it doesn't mean I am going to use it to frighten or control her, that a helicopter overhead is not going to chase her. I've learned she will eat trees, will consume their bark, eat bushes and fences, and pull up Southwestern yucca plants to eat their roots. Now I wrap trees carefully and keep watch on them.

Burros, donkeys, originate in Africa, constantly roaming, eating everything in their nomadic journey together. She has the intelligence to think things over. Others call those moments of thought "stubbornness." But watching her, I am certain she meditates. She watches and listens. Thinks. She has mindfully observed an ant or other insect at times. I still try to learn what I can do to occupy her time, to keep her involved.

In any case, she is another part of the land, a great friend to the mustang, sometimes more of a foal, giving Misty love bites on the fur, later chewing her tail and mane. She is an alarm clock for her feed, knowing the time. But she has not forgotten her early wild life. At times her own genetic memory sends her wandering away from us outside our first pastures, nothing another horse would do.

My Colorado veterinarian recently worked at a mule ranch and he said they are not at all similar to horses, but are still donkeys. Genetically, their behavior is that of a donkey, which reminds me of mixed-blood tribal people throughout the country who still carry ancestral knowledge in their cells.

In our unique tangle and web of kinship and love, both my horse and burro seem now to be part of the spirit of this mountain, forest, and earth where we live, as if we are a part of it all. When I work with them, brushing, or using a medicine, I sing as I do not sing before people. I sing horse songs. The first ones I remember from young days are probably incorrect, but "the girls" don't care.

One always stills them. Some I create new as we work together, as the sweet burro, Raindancer, turns around to have her bottom scratched each time she can receive this luxury, always making me laugh.

The first time she did it, she was still young, gathered from the wild, just rounded up. I thought she wanted to kick me until I realized she wanted only to be scratched. Now I may be cleaning her eyes or face, and she will suddenly turn. She also loves to have her long ears rubbed, inside and out, her prehensile mouth moving as if speaking of the pleasure she feels as I rub the tender softness of her velvet inner ear. Even then, when she's had enough, she turns around and stands waiting for a butt scratch.

It is that the burro, or donkey, has the most logical behavior and sense at that moment. In all her precious, precise intelligence, I am often frustrated about how to fulfill her intellectual needs because I cannot grasp their scope and possibility. Often, with Rainy, I can appeal to her logic. For instance, getting her out of the third pasture before she overeats, it will never work to pull on a rope or use normal means to round her up. But I can explain to her that she will be in danger. She will become sick. Then I wait as she looks at me, considering my facial expression, my mental images, until she finally makes the decision to come with me. In most places, this would never be a way of trying to control or move an equine away from a field of wonderful food, but the two of them are teaching me well. I am touched when the caring Misty pushes the food bin upward and toward me to ease my own labor.

From this radiant life of animals, it is with the ones just outside my home that I have most learned we are all creations of exquisite benevolence, intelligence, and cognition of many kinds. In these bodily creations, our inner lives remember the laws of nature many have long obeyed from sources coming from all the wisdom people, a god that has no name, not Christian, Hindu, Jain, Muslim, or Jewish, but each god the same.

Even the buffalo were enchanted by the wild horses running across earth in their new freedom, as if remembering they shared a muscular, powerful presence together in the dark caves long ago when humans were merely stick figures.

Some of us have watched a herd of wild horses, crows flying above them, as they run across the grasses of earth, down ridges, up hills, almost transparent in sunlight and clouds of dust. But transparent is what they are becoming as they disappear so quickly from the land, so invisibly from most human eyes. We all co-evolved together in so many ways, a part of us needs the great earth energy in the herds as they pass, taking with them a large part of ourselves.

Bear

The bear is a dark continent
that walks upright
like a man.
It lives across the thawing river.
I have seen it
beyond the water,
beyond comfort. Last night
it left a mark at my door
that said winter
was a long and hungry night of sleep.
But I am not afraid; I have collected
other nights of fear,
knowing what things walked
the edges of my sleep,
and I remember
the man who shot
a bear,
how it cried like he did
and in his own voice,
how he tracked that red song
into the forest's lean arms
to where the bear lay weeping
on fired earth,
its black hands
covering its face from sky

where humans believe god lives
larger than death.
That man,
a madness remembers him.
It is a song in starved shadows
in nights of sleep.
It follows him.
Even the old rocks sing it.
It makes him want
to get down on his knees
and lay his own hands
across his face and turn away
from sky where god lives
larger than life.
Madness is its own country,
desperate and ruined.
It is a collector of lives.
It's a man
afraid of what he's done
and what he lives by. Safe,
we are safe
from the bear
and we have each other,
we have each other
to fear.

For Smoke
For Hawk

The Daily Hours

When I carry early morning hay to the horses, many crows are there, clawed feet and legs standing stately and wide on their temporary province of land. Large numbers have drifted down to find the seed and grain that pass through the horses. It is a feast for them in their early search through the manure, while nearby are songbirds doing the same, some frantically throwing it into the air as they search for grains. Much undigested food passes through the bodies of the horses, providing a banquet for these birds, rabbits, and other lives.

When I step forward, the entire field of crows rises up in a cloud of shining black bodies and wings, obsidian blue-black all crying out as they lift up and fly in one darkness of cloudy motion. Their wings all at once create a great noise.

Left behind, the magpie cousins, blue light on their black feathers, continue to work unperturbed. One flies to the back of the older horse. They have formed a relationship, as an elk sometimes does with a bird. In fact, the healthiest elk is groomed by its bird partner. Both benefit from this friendship as the bird eats ticks or other insects.

When it is time to grain and brush the horses, then rake, shovel, and bag the manure, it is never an unpleasant chore. Most would not think of it as poetic labor, or one having its own kind of beauty, but the rich horse manure attracts many lives. Raking and shoveling allow for my attention to everything present. It becomes a meditation. In the decomposing is also the composing, and it is a time to consider the fine qualities of food that has passed through the large bodies with more than enough richness for other lives.

In the morning routine of life here, the world is a large nest where winged animals feed. Robins arrive, no longer migrating south as they once did. Last year, a few mountain bluebirds reappeared, their own fast-beating hearts arriving here, and by now the crows have recognized my face, returned awhile, then passed on through their flyways to their daily unknown locations. Numerous other winged birds have flown in. I hear the wingbeats of the early morning chickadees and feel the breeze of others flying to seeds and grains. Redbirds come from beneath the low, dark bushes for the most shy sustenance from the field. Some settle in to a single location.

I know that during the night, other animals have been here: pack rats, and larger animals, all ransacking manure. How many small beaks or tiny, pink clawed animal fingers have scoured this tabletop of a field I can't know.

This year an unusual species arrived, possibly because of the long drought and intense change of climate. They created a nest outside the door, where I could watch at eye level. At first, they left each time I was near, but soon they became accustomed to my intrusions. I had placed seeds, fruits, worms all outside for them to no avail. I thought I saw only the female, and she had a dark tail, an orange beak, and sharp, black shining eyes. A gray body with yellow chest. The nest seemed sloppy and unusual, built on the drainage pipe. I searched for the name of this bird, finally finding it was a kingbird flycatcher. The female perched quietly on the eggs and rarely left. She was completely silent. I waited, watching for eggs to appear in a nest that at first didn't seem very deep until I thought it was a wintering nest, near the warmth of the house, not one with a clutch of eggs. Then one day a large baby appeared. It seemed already full-sized and able to fly. It flew to a nearby tree where the entire family of hatched and grown birds sat together on the limb. Soon they flew out to the manure. Above it was a sensible place for a flycatcher to find numerous meals.

There is a reason why I often call this a place of *angels and dung*. Other wings appear like visions after the birds leave. In early summer, insects and the flying small arrive, lavender-blue butterflies that have just been freed from anthills. These are most interesting to me, lives coming from inside earth. These have been cared for by the ants while they were cocoons. Some say they are kept in special rooms ants create for them where the immature caterpillars wrapped in their silk robes are pampered by the ants. The ants enjoy a sweetness given off by the undeveloped lives and so they often allow the larvae to eat the eggs ants usually fiercely protect; the sweetness given off by the maturing cocoons is delicious and intoxicating to them. As the butterflies mature and grow wings, the ants with their busy legs open earth, giving the lavender-blue insects the freedom of air and light and the ability to fly away and become a living part of sky. They have had a life of mutuality and coexistence; order in a world considered one only of competition and survival of the strongest. Their lives together, their shared dreams in darkness, offer something of hope that we may one day find cooperative ways of being with other lives, even with one another.

The released butterflies find their first nourishment from the moisture of manure, where they suckle, wings opening and closing like waves of blue water, currents in the river of air. With wings held together like thin paper I wish they'd have written the mystery of their dark winter held in earth. I want to know their unknown story, life in total darkness, life with ants, then sudden light and air, their history with another species of inner earth as parents and caretakers.

Next the painted ladies arrive in their time, with flaming orange and black wings, covering small plants. They fly from branches above the fence down to the manure. The colors of their wings ignite the world with flame. Then they, like others, pause on what is moist and rich as if to imbibe in a wealth of feed. Honeybees join them, bees endangered now in the world. They, too, take in this fertile nourishment, the wine of horses.

Later the perennial bushes in the horse pasture open with their yearly sweet-smelling white blooms. As if color is a cue, thousands of white butterflies immediately appear. The field is again changing with the new. On that first day of summer a storm of flowers looks like winter snow.

It is a constantly transforming world. We living all have our ways to survive. Even the mane and tail hairs of horses are used by the birds in their nests. Reapers and gleaners all.

One morning, shoveling, I find a large pupa inside the manure. It is a gold-colored life of some kind and appears to be growing yellow wings. I don't know what it is, this new life forming. It is not a butterfly. Instead of killing or bagging it, I cover it and remember that one spot, and not to shovel there again. I leave just enough manure behind for it to live on, enough, too, for future earth, steadily seeping its nutrients into the plants that grow with it as earth breathes and yields, gives and gives more.

Another day I find tall, very slender mushrooms growing along the edge of the field, out beyond the fencing. White. Gray. They rise gracefully and thin, nearly invisible. The tops are small and almost as transparent as the negative of a photograph, an intimation of what a world without color might be, yet they are more beautiful than color, more of a brushstroke in Chinese painting or a word of poetry in calligraphy in yet another language I cannot read. Later, I dream about this mushroom and its delicate, thin artwork.

Much of the time, this is a field with hoof and wing, the creature lives some might find disgusting, but truly are a great attraction of beauty as each new life flies in with wings the stained-glass light of sun. There are wasps and the celadon-green butterflies, the lacewinged nearly transparent, all drinking and eating here. A small, fine dismantling takes place. At night, dung beetles burrow into the world outside, making round balls of feed for the future, navigating by constellations and the Milky Way. These many organisms are all citizens here, all mountain walkers.

One early fall morning spider silk spins down from the trees. All around me are their long shining strands, intricately woven webs, fine nets for catching flies. It's a perfect place for them because thousands of flies come to manure, lay eggs, reproduce.

I can think of no tribal nations or stories that don't reveal great care for spiders. They are a part of creation stories and these carry an ethic, sometimes merely about paying attention to the small, but they are also teachers, teachers of weaving and other skills. For us they carried fire across water for our warmth and for cooking when all the other animal people failed at the task.

I watch the spiders where they are suspended in a watching silence. With eyes that move, they wait in stillness for insects. I've watched some leap, capture, and instantly wrap an insect with their finely spun silk. In sunlight, the strands shine around this small world. This is one more creation on earth that inherently knows how to live.

It is a marvel to me how such a small thing as grass creates such large muscle and strength as a horse. The girls, as I call them, are large walking plants made of grasses, oats, sunflowers, and grain, but what comes of it feeds so many others in that fellowship with all the others.

The horses are outside my open windows. We speak to one another, especially in the evenings. I sit where they can hear. They are beautiful, shaking their manes, animals that smell of herbs and earth. Oh horses, the great Mandan warrior said, My God is the horse. In truth, for him, his life in the past depended on the horse. It was the animal that allowed the Plains people to survive after the buffalo were killed. The massacre of bison made horses indispensable, allowing the people to fight for a way of life, for their land, and to hunt for food. The people's continuing survival was the reason Americans later killed the Indian horses, thousands at a time. How fortunate that some escaped. Some of them. And some of us.

Now, as we all grow older, these horses are my companions. Yes, they might be gods in this quiet world because they attract so many other creatures with wings and claws, feathers, bear feet, paws. It is a world of fecundity, seeds, life all around. Here there is wonder and special meaning to life in merely one brief season. It takes all my attention. It takes a great love for the fields and valleys, desert and mountains, and of this beauty so great it is an ache in the human. How easily I could miss seeing or knowing it, but I never want to be a stranger to this land or the lives here. I don't want to lose whatever is natural in my own self, if only it is observations of butterflies or any of my own small actions of caretaking the earth, of shoveling manure each day or watering my drought-dried plants.

At night, standing at the fence with the horses, I hear the owls and sometimes a mountain lion whose loud scream captures the immediate, protective instinct of the mustang who is the head mare and first safe keeper of all us others. I send the lions away by frightening them with a poacher's light. Sometimes I see only their eyes, but at other times I watch their elegant bodies become smaller as they back away. This is for their own safety. If they continue on to town, or kill a dog, trackers would be hired to kill them. Some nights I hear dogs I can't see because sounds travel strangely here, bouncing off stone, traveling down the creek bed or through the canyon, but I know a predator is out there and the dogs speak it.

One sunny day I take a break from raking and sit on the earth, soon to be joined by two young deer. We are on the same earth together in silence. I do not move. I was just sitting on the ground near the horses as they ate and the other animals came along. Perhaps, after so many years, they know me. Maybe it was my silence, or maybe I have been changed to another presence, enchanted by my life here. Perhaps I have become a changeling, as in old stories. For a moment I am not the ordinary enemy.

The Wolves

The day they arrived I first saw the wolves from the window. They walked so silently into my life that the moment I saw the five ghostly presences pass through a storm of snow, I whispered the name, *Wolf,* as they passed by. Wolf is the forest. Wolf is winter snow, dark night. It is red blood on the frozen shine of lake. An animal creation of golden eyes by daylight, brief green fires at night, and fur rich as the gentle drift of snow as it flies up around them. That day it was a wind with silent feet crossing the snow-blinding whiteness of early spring.

They emerged from the invisible, as if coming from inside the hillside, walking silently across a windblown ridge. The wind blew snow clouds up around them. They seemed calm, as if they'd known all along there would be such protection by the elements.

Like a curious deer behind trees, I went to another window to watch them move across earth the way a constellation of five stars might cross the night sky in darkness. Sharply awake inside the fur valuable to themselves, there was no hesitation in their movement.

I watched carefully and kept track of their direction. On this land I am one of the animals, but I try to be one who cares for and maybe even knows the rest, where they are, and what they may do. I watch over an adopted wild mustang and horse, the daily deer herds, and even many wild plants. I care for the snakes as for the little fawn curled when tall grasses are green and new. This is the last remaining wildlife corridor in the region, so I note when the elk bugle, the time of day a certain fox crosses from one hill to the other, when crows see a predator and group together to send it away. Attention is the necessary act, and it is one from which we all benefit. It's important to know where the mountain lions live and how their territory follows the changing curve of land, the creek bed on one side and on the other, past a moss-covered springhouse down the hill and up a high road until hidden above the old town church across the way.

That day it was the pack of wolves I watched travel. They went around a curve of land where no one lived, into fog between hills and canyon walls. Few animals or humans walked there because it was a complicated land and, I hoped, safe. Then there was no sign of them, as if they'd vanished into the invisible from which they emerged.

I hoped the wolves would remain away from any location that would become the crosshairs of their deaths. For many, the word *wolf* carries a dark and heavy meaning. Four letters have made them into something other than what they are and how they resonate inside the mind of many humans. Traditional Native peoples, however, have lived with wolves and recently have even requested their return to reservations. For us, the word means cooperation, a natural connection with the lives of a forest, communication, and loyalty to others. A pack of wolves also bespeaks the health of water, trees, and survival for other animals. For millennia, observation in shared territories has taught us this; the wolf is given an earned measure of respect.

Numerous stories exist about how the wolf helped and taught First Peoples. The wolf is considered a sacred animal. A star is named for it, a constellation. For the Pawnee, its path is that of the Milky Way. For us, it was a leader and we followed the white wolf dog out from a place of conflict to one of peace. Along the way it healed the injured and sick. The beautiful white wolf took us across the river and to a home of peace.

A man named Joseph Little Coyote once told us, at an indigenous science gathering, that the wolves remembered songs for their people who, during the intensification of wars against the tribes, were being chased by the cavalry into Indian Territory. Wolves maintained songs for the people who finally returned to their homeland.

From our mythologies, beliefs, and stories, we've learned to admire or to hate the same beautiful animals, although the hatred and fear are rarely founded in reality. Rarely do most see the true lives of wolves. Seldom do we see the animal stretched out asleep, breathing, or at play with littermates, a mother caring for her young. And perhaps because of this, we live once again in the midst of war against wolves, even those we've restored to the wilderness in order to bring back health to the environment.

Because there are so many ways of envisioning the lives of these animals, for some, the word means to trap or kill. It means an animal of danger, or merely a fur. A killer doesn't consider how quickly life can be taken but how it is never brought back. The name of an animal that cries out for solitude summons these visions not anchored in truth.

As for me, years ago I was in their north, thinking of the paths of their feet over frozen, singing lakes. The landscape where they hid so beautifully was also one they helped preserve. By keeping elk and other animals on the move, they also kept safe trees and willows that were not grazed or eaten, kept them safe for the future, for spring songbirds in the willows, for the beavers and the numerous plants and animals that survive only because of that wolf presence.

In that year of the wolves, one cold windy day in the deep silence of snow, I was preparing to go to work. The dog barked and didn't stop. He was normally quiet and yet I didn't pay enough attention until it was time to go out in the freeze and feed "the girls" with icy hair on their equine faces. Carrying the grain buckets toward them, I saw a great spread of red blood across the snow where they stood. Quickly and with fear, I removed my gloves and examined every richly furred inch of their winter coats, their sturdy legs, bare hands touching their warmth from top to bottom and back again. Both were safe and uninjured. They stood calm and comfortable, relaxed, and ate with great appreciation.

The wind had blown strongly across the snow leaving no tracks, no sign of struggle, but the blood was bright on the snow. I looked around to see where it might have come from or gone, and through the whiteness of that day, I saw spots of that life color outside the fence, so I climbed between the wires. Through the wind, snow above my boots, I crossed the creek and up the hill to the other side. There I found the deer remains, now nothing but fresh pink bones with many teeth marks, a little more blood, and still no prints; the wind had swept white snow across itself.

I knew it wasn't a mountain lion or the deer would have been dragged off to its own place. It wouldn't have eaten the deer all at once. I wondered most why the wolves had killed the deer and not the horses as ranchers might suspect, especially when the deer had much less meat. Since wolves can eat twenty-five pounds at once, this question passed through my mind.

Having quickly eaten, they were gone. For a time I saw nothing of them. I never heard that intriguing howl rise up an octave like a loon that must be related, at least by song.

Time passed. I came home one day to find that I'd interrupted a second kill. A large female elk stood near the horses, her neck wounded and bleeding, but not enough to suggest an artery was opened. I didn't want to frighten her with my approach. All I could do was keep watch. She remained with the horses, mostly on the far side of the shed, until she healed and one day was gone.

No one else sighted these wolves but I would never forget their majestic presence after they journeyed on. They'd traveled a long distance from the Yellowstone fire to arrive at this place. But it was not long before one was killed by a car miles away on the highway. Suddenly wolf presence created a flurry of excitement and scientific commotion, with great surprise that they had wandered so far from their original burned territory.

Wolves have inhabited every environmental niche, and once lived on most all continents where indigenous people, as I said, honored them and their place in the environment.

Destruction is not their way. Nor is random killing, but now those packs that are ravaged and destroyed, their natural hierarchy is broken. It is our own human actions that have created wolves that fit the stereotype and attack livestock.

Once shooters enter the scene, a natural way is broken. Wilderness areas disrupted in this way results in the behavior humans want to alleviate. Instead we've created this circle that begins with rifles and traps.

Cristina Eisenberg, wolf specialist and scientist, kept watch over a pack that was restored. The alpha female was strong, and with all her muscular weight, could hold down and drown a moose, killing it quickly compared to what we imagine to be a long, drawn-out struggle. When this female and her mate were shot, the pack lost its order. Without their elder teachers, the young had no one to pass on intelligent hunting. Hunger drove the remaining younger wolves to kill some cattle. It was human behavior that created the unwanted consequences. We do not always know the outcome of our behaviors. We might not have known that to eliminate a wolf brings destruction, in many ways, to our own environment.

Years after the wolf snow, I related the activities of the wolves in our region to a neighbor. He said he was in Yellowstone when the wolves were restored. He felt good knowing they were in their own territory and that they had later come down to our region. It made him feel somehow a part of their return. Feeling good about their return, we didn't talk about the new "war" on wolves that was beginning in some states.

For me, the wolves entered my life and left just as silently. I never saw them again. The snow disappeared. Green buds emerged from the trees. Plants rose up from the ground. The weather became warm. I worked in the garden, my yearly pleasure.

I could have forgotten about the wolves, but one spring night, sleeping with my windows open, strange noises woke me. It sounded like breaking. I didn't know if a large animal was walking through the trees or if it was a human intruder. Finally, I realized it came from across the creek where the bones of the deer had remained. I got up to shine my bright light in that direction, then turned it off as I realized it was the sound of biting on bones, a bear hungry out of winter sleep, eating the bones, breaking them open, looking for any fat still inside.

I didn't turn on the light. Instead, I simply listened with a smile, knowing that all of us are here and we are breathing the same mountain rarified air.

Dawn for All Time

The moon is filling, a bowl of earthlight remaining in the first of dawn. Venus is near Earth in its orbit behind the black branches of a tree where a large bird sits. Morning arriving.

Standing with others, we smell pine smoke, hear the whispers, and gaze toward the mountains.

And then it is blue dawn. At the top of the mountain is a deer, large antlers. No, that of the antlers is a man. They are one as he wears them. He stands, majestic and powerful. Smoke rises from behind the mountain in dark gray clouds. It smells like the history of pines. It is the odor of ancient places, old trees the deer and the gatherers walked beneath. At the crest of the next mountain, another deer with antlers wide and great as old branches takes my breath away.

For thousands of years this has been a moment of awe, this holy beauty. They come down the mountain, sticks in their front hands used as forelegs of the deer, walking in graceful, animal movement. As one comes to a patch of snow he moves to the side, around sage, mesquite, and walks beautifully between stones. From out of the silence of the morning, there are suddenly the calls of all the animal world and then the other animals come from behind the mountains, around them, crying out with all their strong life. Drums begin, sounding as a heartbeat, and the old men sing, wrapped in many-colored woven blankets. From an old adobe building, the sacred deer mothers are brought out, untouchable by human hands. They walk out, accompanied, and take their place in a row of those standing, the drummers, the elders. They are solemn and with heavy and old grace.

Then the dance that has been here in the long past for over thousands of years begins once again, at one more dawn. The animals and the hunter dance, all of them with reverence and awe on their faces. Elders watch on the sides to be certain all is correct and all are well, and the Pendleton and Navajo blankets are beautiful, standing with their human beings inside them. The people have done this for thousands of years, since before any written history, and they will do this for all the tomorrows.

I am a Native woman, a Chicaza from the Southeast people who were removed from our homelands during the Trail of Tears. We dwell now in the place once called Indian Territory. It was then created for all the indigenous peoples of this continent by the American government. At the time, all tribes were going to be placed here, in Oklahoma, and a wall built around the borders so no Indians could escape. Black Kettle's band was pursued for so many years that their attempts to escape eroded a path of land at what is now Goodland, Kansas, and a highway comes through that path.

In spite of those many of us who have been moved and despite attempts at acculturation, we Native peoples in Oklahoma have, for the most part, maintained our languages and for some, the ways, knowledge, mythologies, and other depths of our old world and homelands. Some "outlaws" retained the songs and dances even though these were illegal, banned by the American government. Because of some I remember, I think much of the traditional mind and intelligence remains, even if it is not like the Pueblo dances, which have been on the same lands unchanged for thousands of years.

Our own lands are now plowed, covered over with asphalt, looted and broken. Still, I look at the language and find in it the way we understood our world in the original homelands, the way a people's view was at work before the tear in our lives. The term for animal, *Nan okcha*, means all alive. It means more than only that which is animated. Embedded in the language, it says that the animals have lives and being and are sentient, as is now related by Western science. Animals, like plants, are a significant part of a whole. They have relationships and connections with other lives. They have different kinds of knowledge and ways of knowing. In the traditional worldview, we have awe of them and an obligation to keep *all alive*. This is part of our human purpose here. Our ancestors survived in order for us to live and we have a debt to them as well. The debt is a moral one, a way of being with this earth and all its inhabitants, all sacred.

The long histories of invasion and conquest have changed cultures, created the extinction of peoples and languages, cleared the forests of medicines that would have been significant now if not for this breaking and the many losses. Still, these cultures remain in regions once thought to have nothing of value. Now we face other challenges shared by all people as polar ice melts and Native villages are flooded and moved, as mines and fracking use up the aquifers. Forests are cleared and the water disappears from cloud forests or even those where I lived in Oklahoma. When water leaves, it has to move to other lands, creating floods, hurricanes, and tsunamis that endanger and kill the inhabitants of those places. And where those forests once existed are now areas of surprising heat and drought. Life is disappearing through the hole we have created that grows over our shared world.

What we don't know about this earth is still large. Old knowledge that we need to learn anew is leaving us. In this changed world, the regard for life is now often missing and our work is in learning to bring it back.

When I consider how we have unbalanced our world, changed its tilt by damming the waters, we have created the opposite of creation. Because of the many changes, another part of what we are charged with is to remember. Writer Meridel Le Sueur called it re-membering the dismembered.

Re-member. I want to remember this land, remember the plants are alive and speak with each other. They tell one another when they are under attack by using a language of chemistry and hormones, as if that is their first language. We must remember songs the plants taught us, about when the corn grew its first tassels, its silken hair with the odor of fresh earth, its new husk growing secret and hidden kernels. I want to remember the green cedar when it first rose up through earth against gravity, to remember the birth of an oak breaking open the acorn to release its first tendril. All beginnings and all alive.

I want to remember when we had dreamers and they knew the water and its first songs, and how the dreamers found water and medicine for the people. *Nan okcha*. All alive. Remember.

We are participants with the world, with the universe. What we do changes things and we need to remember this as much as we need to persevere this way, not just as islands in our cultures but with all people knowing they are part of it. Somewhere in the past of all people are the deep channels of memory, the water dream, memories of the tender shoots of green and welcome magic of continuing for tall grasses. We need this for our grandchildren and for a future right and good. If we live well, it will welcome us.

So, here we are, at the deer dance at the Pueblo. The dancer lifts his antlers with eagle down feathers in them and the sunlight is full now, as full as this, this body of salt blood remembering what is left to offer this earth, animal, all alive.

He turns like a deer.

This Morning

This morning the doe speaks to her young
outside the window.
I do not know what is said but listen,
their love is great as ours.
If the coyote comes the mothers chase it
hoping more are not behind the trees,
praying to the god of deer.

One Mind

*One should pay attention to even the smallest crawling creature,
for these too may have a valuable lesson to teach us, and even
the smallest ant may wish to communicate with a man.*

—BLACK ELK

We stand somewhere between the mountain and the ant.

—IROQUOIS OREN LYONS

Mallow blooms around me as I stand on the hill trying to remove the invasive burr thistle. It is all purple flower from a distance, but the stem and leaves are thorn up close. Working on the thistles, I am easily sidetracked; one day I stop to watch the muscular power of an earthworm push itself into damp earth. This is land I bought to save from development, but it is a gift for me since something miraculous is always taking place in the mountain valley, on the large hillsides, or even in a small crevice of an incredible earth.

I have been trying to understand the way of the ant, to observe them in new ways. Even as a child, if I saw boys standing around an anthill, I fought for the ants against boyhood destruction. The small creatures have worlds we don't know. As for myself, I can only tell people by way of explanation in my life that I was born the way I am, caring for the world and all its creatures, "the least of these," and leave it at that. Part of caring is observation.

Today is hot. I am sweating in the hot sunlight, but I don't let the weather deter me from watching the black ants walk a trail from inside their large mound, bringing out small pebbles, all round and equal in size. A book by Native American writer Delphine Red Shirt, *Bead on an Anthill*, tells how the ants of her childhood journeyed to the Lakota beadworker locations and took colorful beads to place around their anthills, as if they appreciated beauty and art as much as anyone. She said, as a girl, she went to their anthills and stole back beads of matching colors in order to make rings.

This is the end of my long road where I once wanted to make a gate and place copies of *The Mountain and Rivers Sutra* by Buddhist master Dogen. I wanted to place them in a packet for people to read if they entered. Among many words, it contains these: "Do not doubt that the mountain walks. It just doesn't walk in human time." Like many hopes and plans, this never materialized because of the constant labor of living here.

But as for the ants, I always take time to stop and watch. Today they carry sticks of a certain size and pass the sticks to an ant in the entryway. After watching a while, I, too, offer the doorway ant a stick of that size. It takes my offering. Another life accepts what I give. It is one of the mysteries of the world.

It is not that this is participation with nature or becoming a part of it, but I love the delicate way another species takes the stick from me, as if I am remembered from my previous stops. Isn't it what we want in many ways, being accepted, as if the other creatures validate our being, our kindness?

This mound has existed a long time and I've been watching it. I watch the black ants as the horses graze nearby, or while taking a walk. I observe them after a rain when morning arrives with its fresh odor. I admire their shining black bodies and think of the human dwelling places influenced and structured after the building and creativity of ants. It has even entered into our mythologies, Choctaw, Chicaza, Navajo. Our mounds in the Southeast seem structured this way. We did, after all, climb out of the earth. It's said that those of us who stayed behind became the ants.

E. O. Wilson is known for his studies of ants as well as his work on our earth and the role of humans in this world as creators and destroyers. He is a hero of many. Yet in my research, many other studies on ants began long before his time. I am relieved to know that others have found interest in these creatures in the field of study called myrmecology and from many years of observation.

In the 1930s a man named Eugène Marais wrote about the white ants of Africa. As often with Western-minded scientists, I can't ascribe to the scientific method used or created. Instead of relying on the centuries of indigenous observation and knowledge, he was more invasive. Most people come to think this is by necessity and not by choice, ignoring the hundred centuries that have gone into observation and knowledge. In any case, his conclusions shed scientific information on the ant colonies and their intelligence, or rather some quality like intuition or the connection of minds. He ran a slab of metal down the middle of the anthill. Later, examining each side, he found they were created in perfect accordance with the other side, a mirror image. Each tunnel matched that of the other. "It is the instinct and design," he says, "of a separate soul situated outside the individual termite." His choice of words is important. Instinct could naturally be considered, but the idea of a separate soul that lives outside the individual is a profound consideration and a conclusion that could change our view of humanity, not only ants. Building identical structures on each side of the steel sheet was an architecture of being that is a mystery still belonging to all of us.

Some scientists now say that a single ant colony has the same number of brain cells as a human being. Marais concluded early on that a colony of ants was all one consciousness, but work done that long ago may have been forgotten or overlooked. Still, he already knew that it was possible for a colony, perhaps a group or a tribe, to share the same consciousness.

He also tells the story of African driver ants and their response to human beings, as if, like horses, they can perhaps even read what is inside the human. Driver ants occasionally would swarm through human habitations and consume what was inside: roaches, mice, food, even small animals, unfortunately sometimes even small dogs.

One researcher who Marais knew studied butterflies in their region. On hearing the ants were coming, he placed his collection in an airtight safe. He also had many papers of importance. He feared losing his collection as well as his locked-up compilation of work. Out of fear when he saw the ants swarming like a river toward his home, he decided to fight them off. He used every means to keep them from entering his house: fire, poison, anything he found, including water and acid. But in chemical messages from this swarm to the communal mind, the ants called for help and other swarms arrived to assist them. They came in columns, multitudes from all directions. After his great fight, the man was forced to flee his home as the ants filled it. They covered everything, entering in strong, powerful surges. When he returned, they had managed to eat his research and the butterfly specimens he'd saved in the fireproof, waterproof safe, leaving only the mystery of how they had entered his enclosed, safe spaces. The researcher lost the work he'd tried to safeguard, as if the ants knew exactly what to destroy.

On the other hand, a local woman who had long lived there, on seeing them arrive, opened her doors, opened the cupboards and cabinets. She remained in her house as they entered and swarmed her world. She cooperated and because she was of this mind with the ants, as Marais says, they considered her one of them. They consumed the insects, rats and mice, went through her things, ate what they could find, and left, leaving her alone, safe, her dwelling place cleaned but nothing harmed.

I can easily understand that ants are important in our world because there are numerous ceremonies for and about them. They are a part of indigenous and aboriginal traditions both in Australia and on this continent. I have read about the Green Ant Dreaming and the Honey Ant Dreaming from Australia, but I can't pretend to understand dreamlines and songlines, so ancient on their continent. They are complex and belong to an old, powerful tradition and complex mythology. They are not part of my own tradition and ceremonies. I think these mythologies are often too complex for the mind of an outsider from other cultures to grasp. It has to do with perspective and perception, with how our minds are trained, the embedding of knowledge in language and blood.

As for us Chickasaws, our grandmothers respected the spiders and many clan animals. There may be stories of ants we no longer hold because of the broken history. For the aboriginal thinker, though, we know how the mind is experienced, and that the world is known in a different way. In Australia for over sixty thousand years the land has been understood by the first people. The stories tell, as with all indigenous cultures, that there are no rigid boundaries between plant and human, animal and human, insect and human. The existence of art with a theme of the Ant Dreaming—and there is more than one—is another testimony about the connection between the people and the different ants. As for science, there is a learned aspect; the green ant is the only creature in the world with a sensory organ attuned to earth's magnetic field. In all ways, the intelligence and special qualities of these ants have been observed by the people of a continent for generations.

In other ways, knowing the manner of ants is important to humans. As I study, I find that before a bushfire, certain ants put quartz on the side of their hills for protection, and when the people see this quartz brought upward and placed, they know it is a warning that fire is moving in that direction along the bush. The action of ants saves human lives, as well.

I first became interested in the Red Antway because I saw a copy of one of the sand paintings from this ceremony in a museum and marveled at the enormous amount of work, skill, and time that went into such an event and the art associated with it. I had never seen such beauty, the colors slowly sifted by hand, intricate images painted in sand for a temporary purpose before being destroyed.

My sister friend and I are a bit at odds about the Navajo Red Antway, yet she is Navajo. I read that this is a ceremony for men returning from war. She says it is for red ant bites. Yet I think the bites must be a common occurrence. Why would someone pay for such a complex ceremony and go to so much trouble unless it is more meaningful than someone being bitten by ants? In deep myth, there are those who were, according to Navajo poet Laura Tohe, alive in the underworld. They were messengers, according to her elders. One woman, seeing that two mounds of ants had been at war, predicted a large war was coming for humans before World War II, Laura said.

The Chantways are complicated and elegant. I cannot comprehend other cultures except as an outsider. Still, another Navajo person tells me this ceremony is recommended by healers for specific diseases. Looking at it from my perspective, a ceremony brings together all the people. An entire community and family appear in support of the patient or person requesting the ceremony. It is no simple thing. Among the Navajo there are many Chantways. It is a traditional system. These ceremonies are extremely significant on this continent. Nothing is asked for, beseeched, except for a person's place within the natural world, their community, and the universe. I confess, this is much to ask. It is seldom thought about as we live our lives daily. Much is given in these ceremonies, sometimes money, gifts to the singer, to the helpers, small gifts and large.

The ants have a loyalty and a symbiosis, a unity wonderful and strange. Their intelligence is a seeming rarity except that we find it everywhere we look in the world. Also, I have been told by my friend Susan that, in Florida, ants build rafts during floods to remain out of water, safe and floating. The unwanted and dangerous fire ants I learned about in Oklahoma, during floods, roll into a single ball together and float, turning and rotating, in that way remaining on the surface and able to turn each side upward to breathe.

There is great value in knowing ants are something of a single organism, able to pass information in ways we don't yet know; that they communicate and work by smell, touch, that they may milk other creatures, tend to their plants and even weed their gardens, but they are also capable of tender caring. This is apparent in the case of the butterfly cocoons for which they have cared over millions of years of evolution. The ants are attracted to one another by sound and odor. The cocoons are buried in ant tunnels. This species includes "The Blues" of our Rocky Mountains, which remain coddled in ant tunnels before growing scaly wings that help them escape from ants when they mature. Those that are grown with ants have a higher survival rate than other butterflies.

In more ordinary life—if it exists—the labor and value of ants are as significant as worms to the soil, something we usually fail to notice. They aerate and loosen the soil, leaving behind important fungi as they decompose wood and organic materials, assisting in both ways for trees and plants to grow.

I have watched Colorado ants for years and even tried to protect them as deer walk on their hills, rain washes them away, snow arrives in a blizzard, and earth freezes. My brother, after a storm, helped me dig out of the road, accidentally breaking down a large mounded anthill created with the inner stick structure. But the ants reappeared as if by magic, until one day they left for an unknown location.

Another day, out where I shovel manure, I find what looks like blue-black sequins. Examining them, I find they are a clump of dead ants. One piece, or group, holds; the other breaks apart in my hand and the ground shines with their bodies, beautiful in design, perfect in plan, lash-thin legs, all there, coal-black shining bodies.

Longing for such spirit with others, we are not unlike ants. It is not about labor. It is about being all together with the rest of a group or community. Now an unbroken cluster of ants sits in a clay bowl on my desk at work. The backs and thoraxes and abdomens shine like coal from deep inside the earth where they lived until a deep freeze, a drought, or even until I unwittingly shoveled them into the light.

The ants, according to those who know them, are not only co-operative, but the intelligence of these insects in some other countries leads them to create clay cathedrals, surprisingly built. They create unique architectural designs, even making landscapes with arches between columns, with gardens and aphids that are like cattle to be milked. E. O. Wilson writes about those who create fungus gardens with a constant temperature they control through their use of leaves and the temperatures of decomposition so that it is always 30 degrees C.

The stones outside their mounds are all the same. Perhaps, as in Delphine's story, they liked the size and shape of beads. I may never know these things but mystery is a constant in my life and I like it. It is a form of the grace and enchantment with which many observers live. When I work on the hillside, the ants climb the stems of the purple thistle, taking in the sweet glue that holds the petals closed until sun and the work of ants open the flowers. It seems all the world wants sweetness. And, after all, I recall that the ants came from the dreaming. One is the Honey Ant Dreaming.

The Foxes

PRAISE TO THE EARTH BEINGS

It is solstice, the return of light. I have been out watching the earth, hoping the newly planted trees will live, knowing that they will not bear fruit in my lifetime, but hopefully someone will enjoy the feast.

Spring has a rich, deep odor; moist soil as life is born underground and unseen before it is fully visible. We sleep and dream at night, or wash dishes and start the garden in daylight, looking at the newly green world. A hawk moth opens its wings too early against the window; somehow it has already emerged from a hidden silk cocoon. Live births arrive from the darkness and inner waters of their mammal mothers. Elsewhere, eggs are arranged in nests. Some birds sing inside the eggs even before breaking out of their shell. Flowers prepare to open. Trees. Life can't help but be called forward. It is a constant, traveling a circle from the genesis and mystery of every being.

One early morning, standing above me on the hillside, outlined by red sky, stands the slender black fox. She isn't watching me. We have lived here in this place so long, she must know this human resident by now, even though I'm sure no other lives would count a woman as part of their true wilderness. None of us seem as trustworthy as deer or horses, but she never runs when I am present.

Driving down the road to the cabin, I've lately noticed the earth appears slightly hollowed out. Then it is clear that earth has been moved aside, but who would have known this hillside holds one of the entrances to her den? The black fox is often nearby, but never do I know where she lives until one evening a red fox bounds down the hill and enters an opening in the earth just above the road. He is smaller than she is, so I think he is one of her young going into an opening hidden by dry brush.

Inside the hill, a tunnel, the burrow into darkness. I look at it, curious, because I do not know what makes up this well-created warren. On the outside, the entrance is almost perfectly round and as solid as cement, yet difficult to see. Slightly away I see what appears to be another den, this one seeming to go beneath the road.

Whenever I work on that hillside, packing invasive plants into a feed bag, I feel the fox with her eye on me. I do not know that she protects new lives as she looks to where I stand in early daylight. She doesn't move. I am in front of her and I am outside her treasure of infant lives, four infants that suckle and grow in secret.

Sometime later, walking nearby, I watch curious eyes peer out from the refuge so perfectly built and hidden. Shining eyes observe this world, now watching another kind of animal walk by. As I pass, I feel I am watching over them like a strange auntie, aware of them looking out beyond their safe refuge in the earth, learning.

As I consider what is in the mind of a fox, what and how they learn, I think of the mother standing, her full and shining tail, black as coal no matter the light. She guards her little ones. I watch the red male, the father. He often brings food, squirrels, woodrats, rabbits. At first, I'd left a few eggs outside, but they are eating well, and the warren has begun to smell. Plenty of dead animals are at the entrance, the smell of death there where they have been tearing into the meat of squirrels, a magpie, rodents. With so much meat, the little ones must be growing quickly. Soon they will take the shape of the mother.

Nature has, or is, something of a passion for life. And so one day, there they are, four more of that nature and passion. The little soft-furred creatures hunker down behind their mother in the road. Two black, as she is, and two of them appear to be calico, which I have never seen before. As the calico grow, they turn into two-toned foxes, part orange like the father, part black like the mother. These are unique and the mother keeps these little ones immaculate even though they roll about in their earth home. They are small and safe behind her, hiding but looking to see what kind of creature I might be among all the others that pass. She knows the kits, as they are called, are safe. At least from this two-legged animal. We have been on this land together for a long time now. I do not know how many years, but enough to almost have trust. In any case, she knows or somehow senses that I will not harm them.

The opening into the den is large but not in a way that makes it wide and easy to enter or even to see. I imagine their domestic inner world, dried roots at the top and everywhere the odor of rich fresh earth. I could burrow into the scent of it and sleep there. One day this will happen, in some way, whether ash or flesh, but for now I am merely observing life; the kits, sinless, perfectly soft, clean-furred though living in earth.

Between the human and the fox is a bridge of stories, tales, and beliefs. This bridge sometimes misses several rungs of reality, sometimes human compassion. Nevertheless, I step across it to the territory on the other side of what I know of the fox. This new bridge is slight and shaky as I cross a bit to the other side of being human. The fox is there, on her side of living. She has no sharp edges, no corners, no lies. These are admirable traits. She may have fear. She may hide, but she has no lies, no corruption or fury or need for power, only for food and the care for her own young. Perhaps she has to teach them to be fierce.

Her fur in late sunlight shines about her head. It is clear by her look as we grow closer to one another that she is calm with life, a new mother wanting only survival for herself and protection for her young. Her earth shadow grows longer at day's end.

Though our realm of being human is believed superior to the fox's, I want a key to her cosmos. I want to open a door to where, so far, at least, no cruelty has found its way in, because in the last so many years I have watched us fall from what they call grace, falling from what seemed a country of some kindness into this opposite place where water was once protected for our children to drink, but is now toxic, a world where some words could be trusted, and I see us falling from a country that once seemed safe and mostly of honest intent, no weapon carried.

She knows I have crossed this bridge. An ear is turned in my direction, listening to the weight of air as I send her a message that this human is harmless. I only wanted to pass this threshold between species, wishing to observe the beauty of other lives around me, the beauty of her life. It may be irresponsible but I want to see and know the lives that have no need for me. It is only my need to know their depth of intelligence and being. I, too, am an animal, but one most fear, including ourselves.

The ear is turned toward me, listening, dark and shining, whiskers like a cat touched by light. As time passes, she relaxes as if reading my thoughts. I continue: I have seen your little ones. I am the one who left eggs for food nearby. Last winter I saw you leap through snow deep enough to hide you, toward whatever animal you heard beneath the white. You leapt so carefully, so crisply, then hunkered down for that one great final leap into snow to catch that small animal. Then you rose out of it with the rodent.

Now it enters my mind, how foxes have been known to sleep in abandoned hawk nests, having climbed a tree like a cat. I've never seen this. I've only heard about it. I wonder if, looking out across the beauty of earth, the four-legged creature wished just once for wings, for a moment to fly, or if it dreamed of flying as it slept in that aboveground nest. But then, its purpose, like that of all the rest, is to live, to survive in its own manner.

And I think of ayas. In these traditional stories from the far North, mostly Cree nation, a character seeks out Foxwoman, or Old Woman Fox, to ask for her wisdom and learn from her special powers. She is also sought sometimes by others who wish to learn medicine or healing. Foxwoman is an elder who offers knowledge. There are stories about her, songs and blessings. Her gift to others is wisdom, passed on from generation to generation. Most often she is something of the special world, not like any of the tricky slyness of Western stories. These prayer songs for and about Old Woman Fox are based on hundreds of thousands of years of observation.

I watch for paw marks near the earthly entrance in the hill, but see none, though they are seen in other places, the pasture where she hunts, on the road, but the full tail may erase the marks and hide the fox from any predators.

This earth is a shining, breathing being. We still know too little about it, but it breathes and moves. Ask the tides. Ask the trees. And from dark space it shines with blue life. I look outside in the morning to see birds in the sun as wings open and they lift away in tidal winds. The crows shine with so many colors few notice, and those foxes up the road breathe in the earth as their father arrives the color of copper, bright in the morning red of sun coming over another mountain like a thin outline of flame.

In the morning, I have a dream; it is a weighty dream and I want to remember it and hold it close to my heart. It is one in which too many lives that were gone have returned, but when I wake I know that the world is changing. No caribou come any longer to the caribou people. Migratory water birds have no water. The world sinks because permafrost is melting. Who was it who said not a single other animal would miss us if we were gone?

Last year was a serious drought. I wonder if the fox prays to a god of its own, for mice and squirrels and the trees I want to protect, for water in the creek. Thinking of the fox I think of how her young will soon pass by at night and each one will scream as they consider their own lives and territories. And this they do. It takes so little time.

The beautiful earth beings. Even the dog does not follow after them, as I tell her not to and she learns. Perhaps the screams frighten her. But when possible she watches every move as they crisscross the pasture looking for rabbits. I know rabbits are there. The signs are on the ground. They know it, too, by smell.

Their exquisite being and the stories about them are an enchantment created of beauty, *encanto*, as these essays began. The fox lives with a kind of enchantment that has been returned to the world. And so it is, with my own prayers to the four directions with cornmeal or tobacco, I sing to these lives in this land of all our wilderness gods.

The Voice of the Crow

Edward Howe Forbush quoted Henry Ward Beecher as once saying that if men wore feathers and wings, very few of them would be clever enough to be crows.

This morning the many shining blue-black crows arrive, so many I can't count. I live in one of their flyways. Some of them are ragged, a wing torn or missing a feather. Some are still in their young perfection.

The crows wake me with their loud pronouncement, saying, *We are here.* Always they announce their presence.

The crows speak wildly and with powerful vocabularies. Sometimes they speak a paragraph. One of them sat on a branch above the horses one day and spoke to me for a long time in a low tone, as if telling a story or delivering a lecture the way ancient philosophers were known to speak like many other lives and beings, this one group of crows has large vocabularies. Once one stood on the rough branch of a tree above the horses and spoke to me, it seemed, in long sentences without ever repeating the same word or sound. I listened carefully to its clicks and language, and I took the words seriously, as if I could understand what was being said as the crow looked at me with its shining eye.

I would like to understand even the smallest parts of their forms of communication. Paying attention is the least they deserve from our own animal lives. After all, we have treated them badly, misunderstanding their purpose, and historically, we've made numerous attempts on their lives.

The magpies are related to the crows and they work together, especially during fledging time.

The crow has been so respected through history that some versions of the Bible have a crow rather than a dove being released by Noah after the flood. The crow did not return and that's how they knew the land was no longer covered over with water. Also, a crow defended Saint Vincent and was shown sitting at his foot in early statues and etchings. They are powerful creatures in world mythologies. In some Alaska native stories, the crow organized the world, as did the mother of God, Sophia, in some versions of the Bible, she telling him how to fit the creation together. For our tribes, the crow was once white but became black when it went over water to an island with a great burning tree in order to bring fire and light back to the people. Crow's white feathers were charred, although the feathers remain with a rainbow of color to light them, dark blue appearing predominant.

This band of crows where I now live moved here after the land by the river was bought by a developer. He claimed to be an arborist when I asked him about the trees, but proceeded to cut all the trees, even those where they'd nested for years. He even cut the rich apple trees that grew in a row and those that kept the land from dissolving into the water.

The crows moved here, perhaps because they recognized me and the horses that were on the large acreage where the buyer's dream existed. Since then, I have never followed them to their nests. They fly along the creek's snaking movement all the way past one spring and into an unknown location. This valley is deep and long and with no other inhabitants but myself and the wildlife. I've followed the curve of creek a long distance and not seen their nests.

Researching the practices of my own tribal ancestors, I recall reading that the crows were welcome in our great gardens and complex sites of agricultural design once the plants began to grow. They ate the insects and pests from our plants. The newly arrived Europeans believed we were lazy farmers because we allowed the birds' presence while they kept them at bay, thinking they ate the plants, although I know it is true that the crows would have searched out the seeds and first tendrils. I've watched them search for sunflower seeds the horses may have missed.

They arrive just before dawn, like the comet that is supposed to be visible in the next weeks. And then they break into groups and pass on to their numerous daylight locations.

Somewhere, down the winding canyon areas, somewhere hidden from our trespasses, they roost for the night. I don't know where they have built their great nests, only that they are known to nest together by the thousands, sometimes many thousands, silent through the night before they set off in their own groups by day.

When the crows are screaming, often it is their call of distress or their attack of predators. I have seen them chase away a fox or another kind of predator, a hawk from inside its hidden site where it stopped to watch for food. An elk calls out as if it is inside the room. I go outside but see nothing. What I find the next morning are two sets of mountain lion tracks jumping over the rock ledge in the snow, chasing the tracks of elk. I follow the tracks, expecting to see the elk down in bloody snow, just as the wolves recently killed a deer by my bedroom and dragged it down toward the creek that runs through this land. But the elk ran with freedom instead of with a predator on its back, and it went toward town. This time, no blood stains.

This is the town that was in national newspapers a few years ago when a mountain lion went in through the French doors of a bedroom that were left open to the night air and took away one of the family dogs while the people remained in bed, motionless and afraid. We live with the beautiful world and in it lives the lions, the other wildlife that don't have maps, don't follow human rules.

While hiking I have found the piles of bones remaining like fossils in the special areas. Most of us have been here long enough to know ways to live with the predators. I have talked them back into the canyon or used a brightly charged light to frighten a lion into backing up to the safety of darkness.

The lions wouldn't have followed any animal into town again, not after trappers were hired twice when they appeared there, and any mountain lion behavior was interpreted as a crime punishable by death, even if it was any cat that was trapped and killed.

At first I am happy the elk hasn't fallen to predators. But there is also mountain lion hunger. Perhaps, since they were a pair, they had young ones. Or it could have been a female teaching her off-spring. But I do not believe they were hungry when I remember it has only been two days ago that a kill was announced by the dark cloud of crows. Perhaps that is the reason they are called "a murder of crows," when they group together and fly to a death. The crows follow the dead and, when hungry, are also known to lead predators to their prey in order to eat leftovers and pick the bones. In that way, they are like the numerous vultures in Oklahoma. You look up to catch sight of them and then follow them to the dead. I grew to care for vultures because I lived in a place where life that didn't earn money was without value to most people. Dogs, cats and their litters, all the animals were picked clean on the road, except for one coyote who mysteriously remained until it was thin hide and exposed teeth. It had probably been poisoned. These birds learn quickly what is deadly to them and they don't eat it.

Crows are marvelous, brilliant survivors. My favorite time is when they land in the field with the horses and manure, picking the undigested sunflower seeds or other grains from the earth. With some invisible signal known only to them, I watch them rise all at the same time like a dark cloud or crow blanket, shining, beautiful, and, at this moment, almost silent. One of these I recognize easily because it has a wing half white, easy for the human eye to follow even when it is buffeted by the wind.

In the physical drama of their world, however, they fledge their young in the wealth of trees near my cabin. Perhaps it is thick and safe here. Their young are noisy and one of my friends says they sound like adolescent brats. They do not want to fly. The magpies help the parent crows. They are in this together, and the young are coaxed endlessly until it seems the adults would tire. It is a noisy time of year as the young complain and whine before finally making just a small leap to another branch.

Later they will enter a stream of wind, the wind like an ocean's jet stream, and the waters it comes from carries so much of the unseen within it. It contains clouds of water from the ocean, the beautiful scent of the balm trees, the dangerous fallout of Fukushima. It is their lifeline. It can also be invisible betrayal.

But when the wind moves them, they journey together like a native family. They follow the path of creek or the possibility of death, the animal who has "kill" on its mind.

When I worked in a veterinary school wildlife clinic, one student asked me which bird was my favorite. At the time, I was feeding a young crow. Thinking over his question, I wasn't sure I had a preference, but he quickly answered his own question, saying his was the crow because they are such survivors. They want to live. The students had better survival rates with them than with the other poor animals and birds that went insane and ignored in the small clinic because students had tests and study and grades to keep up. As soon as he asked me, at that moment, the crow bit me, leaving a bruise. I see what you mean, I said, as the crow ate with great gusto. Some birds won't eat. But the crows, as he said, are determined to live.

A determined bird is something to deal with. Some are determined to eat, some to migrate many thousand miles, or to transform themselves into a newly molted color of feathers, or they design colorful nests of found items to attract a mate who will inspect it before making her decision.

The crow wants to live. That is its determination. And I want it to.

I read a story from some time back and it was about two crows, one with a broken wing. They had arrived at a place of clay in the earth. The clay was a kind that could create the small dishes and fruits I used to make as a child. But one crow, with its innate knowledge, used the clay to make a cast for the wing of the other, to repair the broken wing. How it knew this is a mystery to us. It is a good story, ending with healing. It reminds me of what the old people say, that we learn healing not only from listening to the plants but also from observing what the animals do. The crow was never mentioned in those stories of healing. It was mostly the bear we followed, to learn the plants.

There are moments when I am in kinship with all, seeing into the world and its life, sometimes even the universe. In those unusual moments, we are all one community, the tall grasses, lion, crow, and the human being with language that searches for a way to speak of these moments of the genuine spirit. In these short-lived moments I understand I am only a small human with great lessons to learn from the terrestrial intelligence all around me. But still, I am part of it.

The two crows remained in that place until the wing was healed, the clay removed. When the wind caught the spirit, they left. Two intelligent birds with vocabularies so large I cannot understand them, but I know they do much more than make only cawing sounds. We need the crows and their cousins. Not just because one shows a great love, remaining with another while the cast it created healed its wing, but because our presence is so large it might be easy to forget the knowledge of smaller creatures and how they live together, helping one another.

Their stories allow us to become more human, their behavior teaches us not only our first medical lessons learned, or that they are strong orators, but that we sometimes become too busy to live a life, to listen, to be attentive to the world around us. When in large groups, as they most like to journey, they are a darkness passing over, casting shadows across the earth. They may appear shining black, but to my heart they are light.

Mountain Lion

She lives on the dangerous side
of the clearing
in the yellow-eyed shadow of a darker fear.
We have seen each other
inside mortal dusk,
and what passed between us
was the road
ghosts travel
when they cannot rest
in the land of the terrible other.
Red spirits of hunters
walked between us
from the place where blood
goes back to its wound
before fire
before weapons.
Nothing was hidden
in our eyes.
I was the wild thing
she had learned to fear.
Her power lived
in a dream of my leaving.
It was the same way
I have looked so many times at others

in clear light
before lowering my eyes
and turning away
from what lives inside those
who have found
two worlds cannot live
inside a single vision.

It Walks Away

Because the poem above, "Mountain Lion," became part of an installation in a habitat for twin mountain lions, I was able to meet with the woman who gave two full years of her life to raise, or mother, the cubs. She lived with them day and night in their own environment.

As we walked toward their large enclosure, we spoke about the cats and her work. She told how their new home was created as close as possible to mountain lion environment, including large evergreen trees they could hide behind when tired of the human presence. Sure enough, the place looked familiar to me, a person living in mountain lion territory. Inside are mountains, large stone, and coniferous trees. But they also have a waterfall rushing into a pond large enough to allow them to swim.

Mountain lions are known to be gentle and loving with their own kin, but few of us think about a relationship that might develop between their species and ours. The human mother said that while raising the cubs, she worried about how, in their closeness, she would separate from them at the right time. To her surprise, the lions knew, seemingly from their own innermost selves, what they would have known in the wild; at two years of age they began the process of separation. In spite of this genetic, inborn knowledge, their immeasurable emotion of love for her remained. Independent, they still recognize her as something of a mother. As we approached their environment, they squealed when they saw her, then purred loudly and rubbed against her. She bent to their level. They were together, loving, affectionate, and playful. I was fortunate to see the depth of their love and hear sounds I would never hear in the wild.

Yet with their intelligence, they knew the limits and boundaries of species. She also knew that their reason to exist was not to befriend humans. As much as possible, they needed to retain some part of wilderness. The reason great trees were present for them was to hide behind when tired of our kind.

Those of us who live in wild zones know that wildlife is not meant for us, however we cherish the grace of such presence.

Later I remembered the first time I saw a mountain lion in the wild, long before my life here in Colorado. I lived in the Blue Mountains of Oregon near a rich forest. I was a young woman. One day lying outside on wild grasses reading, I felt the uneasy, chilling sense of being watched. I sat up and looked about, only to see a mountain lion slowly stepping toward me. For a moment, I marveled at the golden muscularity of the feline body, its tawny perfection and grace. Then I realized my vulnerable situation and stood to leave.

When she saw me rise and stand, the lion turned back and walked into the shadowed forest where she was hidden by dark strands of hanging moss as if she'd stepped through a curtain.

More than a decade ago, three mountain lion territories overlapped in our region. A tracker was called in because of the possible danger. One lion, perhaps more, vanished after this. For a time, I greatly missed the cats that traveled through the night, slender and gold, leaving behind only a glimpse of eyeshine.

The population recovered or returned fairly quickly and those of us who had long lived here listened once again to their calls joined with the many other sounds of the lives around us. We knew them, and knew to go indoors if we heard a mountain lion call out in its sometimes woman-screaming or strange cat-hissing sounds. Walking in the woods, we knew to carry our own form of protection: a heavy stick, mace, bear spray. And the next day, there was much conversation about the cat that came through the forest toward us.

At my hidden place, cat calls from the backwoods are eerie and indistinguishable, as are all sounds. The call can't travel a straight line because of the stone walls and geology where rock and hillside cross, moving sound from one place to another. It carries a human voice or animal cry back and forth until no listener can discern the origin. Still, I know to listen and be silent when a mountain lion announces it is somewhere near.

There are nights the screaming sounds assure me something of the wilderness remains here in spite of many changes, even though there are fewer than in the past. Then, with the townsfolk, it was a land where a bend in the road might reveal the horses that freely roamed. A few of us citizens from the earlier days remain, inhabitants who know that a beautiful night creature is stalking what it can. We'd speak about the porcupine we all saw rambling along the road as if she was a well-known friend. We told one another when the colorful Western tanagers arrived for early autumn's purple berries, or the return of mountain bluebirds and any other wildlife that appeared. We kept watch and happily shared stories about our nonhuman residents. It was a close community.

The population has now changed and sometimes, when a cat or other being calls out, many people go outside, talking excitedly, and hoping for a sighting of the animal. Perhaps it takes time to become trained to this earth. Until then, like children, the humans are ignorant of the dangers and have not developed the sense and manner needed to live in a place near a wilderness region.

The dilemma is that we have a human longing for wilderness but it is subtracted by their very presence here. Hoping for a glimpse of a bugling elk or, in this case, a mountain lion, may even cost the lion its own mission of hunting for food. Yet I understand that the vision of wilderness is desired by human beings. It is a need, even being lost to those who seek it. In addition, habitat loss is a threat to wildlife and the large new homes are not like the smaller dwellings of the past.

Now when I drive up my old road and into the town, I see the many cut trees, the mowing of once-beautiful mountain grasses before they have even seeded, changes to the environment more familiar and comfortable for suburban residents. One man cut all his great ponderosa pines, then mowed a hillside of tall grasses in order to mediate against fire, only to have a hill dry and dead, ready to burn his wood home in a flash. At the time, my own untouched region was still green, moist and thriving. We need a better education on how to live with this world.

Many insurance companies even advise the removal of our necessary ecosystems, their agents not having stood on earth so hot it will melt their shoes two weeks after a fire passed through. After watching one fire from my windows, I saw how fire moves, leaping from tree to tree, crossing long distances in a flash of light, moving the way a mountain lion moves.

Now I believe that more than watchers, we have become the watched. We are seen, secretly, quietly. The eyes of the hidden are all about, focused on us, watching what we do and how we live. Above here is a large stone outcropping I often observe, a perfect post for watching life below. I have never seen a mountain lion there. I've felt it, though. I know it's a perfect lookout.

The wild is filled with watchers. Perhaps they wonder about us, this species, or even why we are not as before. Human silence is missing. The world around us moves faster. We seldom watch. Our own observance is now missing. In my novel *Power*, about the loss of an endangered Florida panther, a favorite part is where the cat watches the people, knowing they have broken their original covenant with other living animals of this world, the sacred law given at our beginning. The panther "remembers when humans were so beautiful and whole that her own people envied them." They admired the people who stood with grace and "sang so beautifully." It remembers how, when the humans sang, the whole world rejoiced. As in our past tribal stories, the watching, listening panther is one who gave humans the power of medicine. This is often an indigenous understanding about the large cats. They not only carry mystery but make offerings and gifts to human beings.

On rocky slopes or through the forest, a lion walks silently. On the open page of some mornings I see that a cat has walked through, as if to let this mere human know this is still its own world, leaving prints, large and nearly rounded, in the sand or mud.

Seeing this, the creation of a song comes to me, not a deer song I learned, not the song I heard at the place where my people left for Oklahoma. It was a song that belonged with the lion as it walked by, one with an inner force so strong with feeling it could never be spoken in our words.

In our Chicaza world, the name for panther was *Koi-ikto* (there are varieties of spelling), meaning the cat of god. At times, when the primal sense arrives like wind on skin, the strongly felt presence of a mountain lion, one of us knows the cat of god is near. It is that unmistakable feeling and from so mysterious and powerful a being as that of earlier times, when the panther appeared painted and etched in caves, some reached only by canoe, when it was a cougar in petroglyphs in the Southwest, arborglyphs in California. It is known also as lynx in the North. The cat is a strong force throughout the world, acknowledged since earliest times.

Here, in many ways, the lion *is* this place. Its story has remained through a century or more of mining and other changes in the past. And, like all the rest, it sees us.

One recent night, a friend and myself were driving home, when what crossed before us at the far end of our road was a lion, large but lithe, tawny grace itself. It looked at us and it was a stopped and magic, slender moment in our lives as we also watched in silence, neither able to speak. It was a moment in the spiritual creation of this world. After it walked away, we could only sit in silence as if something of great importance had just taken place. It did. We felt it. The cat, the wilderness that remains. It was an event that might sometimes hold a hint of fear combined with the overwhelming amazement at their beauty, a tawny slippage like water sliding behind stone canyons and into forest darkness. All sacred animal gods walked through that stopped moment in time, shadows walking across the valley and into the forest, the woven-together whole of this one wilderness. *Nan okcha.* All alive. The word for animal.

It knew we were there. It stopped and looked at us. We were harmless, the eyes said. We were silent. It merely walked away.

Revelations

*The events in our lives happen in a sequence in time, but in
their significance to ourselves they find their own order . . . the
continuous thread of revelation.*

                                                    —EUDORA WELTY

Years ago, when I first moved here, the surveyor quit. He said
he'd come across a nest of rattlesnakes, and it was too dangerous.
I didn't know if snakes were really there, but even if they weren't,
this mountainous land is admittedly also hard labor. I'd followed
the original owner to all the points of his known and remembered
land. Climbing hills was the easiest work, but we also needed
to scramble over large fallen trees, scale large stones with barely
a handhold, and pass through fallen piles of sharp rocks where
snakes could possibly have lived. Passing between trees, I'd already
discovered from hiking here that it was not easy. The owner warned
me of large floods that I believed were probably events only of the
past and he told me about the mountain lion that had circled and
watched his sons at least one time. He said nothing about snakes.

In nearby towns, or driving backcountry, I often notice the rat-
tlesnakes and bull snakes stretched out across asphalt or our dirt
roads. Most people try to run over them. They are one creature
disliked, even hated, and seen as without a place in the world. But
when I see them stretched there, warming in the sun and looking
like a long stick or the shadow of a fence post, I stop the car to go
chase them from the road. Once at the side, they usually disappear
into the grasses or brush, making a sound as they travel through
and separate the plants as they journey quickly away.

Bull snakes and especially rattlesnakes are becoming scarce now, not just here, but throughout the country. This isn't just because of that fear of them.

These beings have figured strongly in world mythology, biblical stories, and numerous histories of the sacred realm. In our Southeastern tribal archeology, they were guardians who held up the four corners of the world. In the European past, serpents were important symbols of healing and valued medicines, the reason they remain even today on the doctor's staff.

As I mentioned elsewhere, the most far-reaching astronomical animal across tribes throughout the continent is the great horned serpent, a shape-shifter for us that is sometimes also associated with an underwater panther, as well as the plumed serpent of the Maya. According to the mythologists, the snake goddess is also the goddess of waters. She appears often in ancient Greek and Minoan carvings as a woman with serpents wrapped about her arms or body.

The snake predictably represents immortality because of its ability to shed its old skin and reveal a young, bright, and alive new body. I have picked up their skins. The thin shed scales are an intact and perfect semblance of the original snake self, even with the eyes appearing intact.

Despite all the symbolic representations of the past, primarily I think of snakes in their contemporary presence, even though at night I still do see the one that crosses the sky. Besides that, another that comes to mind from my childhood in Oklahoma, where many snakes were plentiful, includes a black racer I carried home when I was a girl, thinking I'd found the best worm for fishing. This one didn't fit the category of an ancient goddess, but was real, lightly scaled, beautiful, and darkly slender, perfect in all respects including my happiness at discovering it. It had been in the stones of an abandoned well and was too beautiful for me to imagine placing on a hook for fishing. I was proud of my find, though it turned out to be an unfortunate one, frightening my mother, harmless as it was.

I most strongly recall a sighting years later. I was out hiking with my dog, Annie. As we moved quickly uphill, Annie stopped her joyful run in the dirt road and stared upward, completely still. I followed her gaze and saw a great golden eagle flying with a large snake in her talons, both shining gold in the sunlight, the snake writhing in the eagle's talons against the deep blue sky. We both remained watching as the eagle carried the snake through sky, over large trees, until both soon vanished.

At the time, I worked with eagles and other birds of prey. Sometimes a snake entered the flight cages. It never occurred to me that it might become prey. Nor did I think of them as creations who would attack the birds or even myself. I mostly admired each of them for a while, their color or pattern and smooth, fluid movement. Then I used a broom to send them out the way they'd entered. They were simply other animals who'd come into the large enclosures to eat the food placed inside for the eagles, owls, or the other birds who had to fly down to catch rodents or even the rabbits in order to prove they were capable of being released. After their trial, they were taken back to the places where they'd been found injured or caught in a fence with a bad or broken wing, cuts, or other damage that usually originated from the human-created environment. Most often, their mates had waited for them and they eventually flew off together, leaving us overjoyed.

It was probably the same shared desire for a mouse or packrat that caused my cat to be bitten with the needle-thin fangs of a rattlesnake early one afternoon. Before I knew what happened, I saw the snake. It was so unique in color and design, I picked it up to examine and admire its beauty before it slid away from my hand and glided off around the corner of the hay barn. It had no rattles and was quite fat. Its markings were unusual, beautiful as African cloth, with dark brown and black dye on a creamy white background. It had no diamond-back markings or anything that looked like the venomous snakes I knew to stay away from. Fortunately, at least for me, it had no venom left. And unfortunately, its toxin had gone into the leg of my cat, Sunshine. It never occurred to us that it was a snake bite that made her so sick, not until the vet shaved her white leg for an IV and it revealed the fang marks. Scratches were on the leg above them, as if she'd either tried to attack the pain of her own leg or the snake had tried more than once. Venom is not only sharply painful, but even worse, as she lay on her side, it caused her organs to close down little by little, and life slowly began to escape the body of this beloved cat with black fur around both eyes like a mask, making this little calico look a bit like a raccoon.

Sunshine was a stray cat I'd brought back from Oklahoma. She'd been small and lived in a back alley where other cats attacked her, competing for food. I remembered sleeping with her the first night I rescued her from the alley and the attacks that kept her from the food. Now I also remember how, once medicated, dead fleas fell like pepper all around her on the rug. I'd held her close as we slept. The next morning, she finally opened the clawed flesh around her eyes and they were a surprisingly bright blue. I said, "Good morning, Sunshine!" That became her name, and for several years it was also her world as she insisted on sitting outside on a ledge of stone in the Colorado sunlight.

Curious about why the rattlesnake had no rattles, I looked it up and discovered that this was a phenomenon seen across the country. The theory given was that they were becoming extinct and it was primarily because of the rattling warning that gave away their locations and led to their deaths. Losing their rattles gave them the chance to remain in hiding and escape hunters who went out to find and kill the large numbers in their dens. I knew Texas and Oklahoma had yearly rattlesnake roundups where people killed the largest possible numbers in contests that were sponsored by nearby towns. They'd disappeared into the silence of death as their skins hung on fences, drying in the sun to decorate hats and other items.

In Oklahoma, there were also yearly predator hunts. I recalled a day I looked for my missing dog. Down a hidden road, I saw an animal the same tawny color as the dog, but he had no response when I called him. Walking toward the animal, wondering if he might be injured, I saw the large mountain lion stand. Mountain lion. It stood so very slowly and looked at me, then turned and walked away as if tired of escaping the guns of humans, fully expecting me to shoot. It walked so very slowly, not sick, not old, just having given up on living. I will never forget that look of hopelessness, almost willing to sacrifice, to have it over. It was a beautiful animal so very tired of human beings. It wanted only for us to go away. It was in a place, a small town, where animals met different shapes of death than elsewhere. They were stolen for labs, used as targets, killed for reasons I can't puzzle through, tossed out on deserted roads or on highways for other slow deaths. Dogs were taken as bait for dogfighters. And the few remaining predators were mostly gone for excited adrenaline-hyped hunters to compete for small cash prizes or trophies. At work, I'd been mocked for my feelings about losing another of my animals. I still heard the mocking words of my boss.

Now, back in a more humane Colorado, I couldn't watch Sunshine die in pain. I asked the vet to come, now, to please put her to sleep, end her pain and her life. I felt broken and I was breaking down just to see her suffer and fall into death. I wept and held her as with one injection her life was peacefully and instantly gone. A gift. I wished we could all be passed from one realm to another in such a quick and easy manner. I knew that, at home, her playmate would cry out for her, and he would miss this friend a long time.

Later, with one of our usual interesting conversations, I told my granddaughter about the rattlesnake without rattles. She is finishing a PhD in environmental studies and had read that the lack of rattles wasn't a quick evolutionary development to save the lives of the snakes, but that because so many fewer now existed, they were mating with bull snakes and no longer developing the cautionary rattles.

I tried to lay straight all the many loose ends of this life: living, aging, one more experience that means I am losing so much around me; friends, family, lovers I once had who are gone now, large griefs, and this last one, Sunshine, the blue-eyed cat who only wanted a mouse.

I considered, too, the many changing patterns in all lives with this world, this blue planet rapidly changing, the climate melting the permafrost, wildlife starving, most of it not understood by humans. And then lives being killed for trophies and other meaningless reasons. Indigenous people are on islands where the sea waters are rising. I have already seen ants, birds, insects, and many others moving farther north in just the space of years, over large miles where stands of trees are dying because of atmospheric changes, and people are drinking water with lead and chemical toxins or waste from factory farming. Worse, in some places the poor are charged coins to operate a well in order to have one bucket of clean water. In some way, one beloved cat fits into the changes of this planet so small and blue from space, all in one overall pattern of loss and change so great and present.

There is no way of tying together all these threads I call *loose ends*, but they truly are ends, in so many meanings of the word. The weaving of our world is not just a changing pattern; the whole fabric is coming undone. Strangely, since then, as if by intuition, the snakes have disappeared. I haven't seen their night writing across the sand, as if they were trying to write a story before morning.

I will miss the sweet cat named Sunshine, but there is so much more, and I believe in hope for a future if we stop now and begin to weave the threads back together, if we no longer permit the destruction of a ten-thousand-year-old den of snakes or learn we cannot change any part of this world by killing, taking, or breaking any small parcel of an undivided ecosystem.

It is clear that we are also losing parts of the soul of the world; I will never forget the slow walk of a dispirited mountain lion, another cat, looking for only a moment at me, her possible killer, as she passed down the road until she was gone.

Kingbird at the Door

Believing forests, waters, plains, even mountains, are all a part of our human genetic code, I've given too little thought to the daylight air and sky. Maybe even to birds along with the wind and currents of air that come from storms in far oceans. Working with birds that were sick or injured, recognizing their feathers, the weight of them, and their sounds, I still never thought about sky as much as I thought of soil, enriching it. When I first noticed the material above the drainpipe by the door of the house, I thought it was a new packrat nest. They are darling animals but last year I could not rid my world of them and they became destructive. One built a nest in the garage with everything it could find, zipping through the alfalfa, carrying the best of it to beneath a stored chair, then the nest grew too large and began to fill the space behind another. It was a beautiful creature, but eventually I had to admit that it could not continue to make its home here. Each day when I laid the horse-feed stirring stick on the metal container, the packrat took it to its large nest. I picked it up only to have it removed again each night. The packrat's droppings soon covered the floor and its teeth tore into boxes stored there. They are sweet animals but able to take over the world around you.

I found only one man who would rid a packrat humanely. First, he said, I would need to packrat-proof everything, making certain it had no way into the garage or house. Then he would capture the packrat and release it in the mines that still existed in Idaho Springs. The miners, for their own reasons, liked having them present.

I went to work sealing every entrance, fixing doors so nothing could enter beneath. I climbed the hillside looking for holes or cracks, never convinced that this intelligent rodent could not find or create an entrance.

In the meantime, it used the best of the feed, built a home too large for its size, took away hats, a glove, anything found. Every day it took the stir sticks used for the horse feed and I would retrieve them. Then another nest began on a beam above the door. I discovered they climb walls. Finally, I gave up and called a pest control number. They weren't humane. The man who arrived climbed up and down the hillside. He found numerous nests. They were everywhere and he left poison near all of them while I tried not to think if I'd caused suffering, but also thought of my life with packrats.

When I saw the sloppy nest on the drainpipe, I was certain it was a packrat, but I didn't have the heart to remove the gray nest. It was made of horsehair, lichen, thin grasses, stems, and dried leaves chewed into lace. It was unlike the nests of the past, but I kept watch on it because it was so close to the door.

One day I saw an unfamiliar bird tail stretching over the back of the nest and I was grateful I'd left it in place. I wondered what kind of bird was nesting here. She was gray with large dark eyes, a long scissortail, and an orange beak. She was undisturbed by our comings and goings, as if accustomed to humans. I rarely saw her fly, although at times the nest was empty. Soon I'd see this unknown bird return, but her flights were invisible to me.

The nest didn't seem deep enough for eggs so I wondered if this bird was settling in for a hard winter. It would be a wise place, warmth leaking from the worn front door, overhead protection from snow, rain, even from the owls that arrived in these mountain forests in January and February, owl mating season.

She looked back at me as I gazed at her black shining eye in what I first thought was an all-gray body—until one day she shifted and I saw that her belly feathers were yellow. I tried to learn the bird that shared my passageway. She was most baffling, according to my bird books. Few of the birds I looked at had the orange beak, and it was the beak that made it difficult to identify. It baffled all my books on birds until I finally found some of these in pictures had orange, as if an occasional gift. No other such nests, and no other scissortails in this location.

The coastal people of the Northwest create art with all animals of an ecosystem within them. Carver and painter Bill Reid once wrote about this in regard to his own work, but I had also seen it in the oldest doorways that were carved as the gentle eyes of seals, bird wings, or whale fins, blowholes, and other animals in their locations. The knowledge of an environment is contained in many indigenous works of art in other places as well, including Cree and Inuit paintings and woodcuts, where sometimes even the contents of an animal's stomach are revealed, as if the work teaches the lives of animal creations.

I wanted such knowledge now, but I also wondered, with the changing climate, if the art was also changing because I was certain this bird appeared from a warmer Southern climate. She was not one seen in a whirl of any similarly feathered beings flying at their daily intervals, but only in a nest of what seemed a solitary life, sitting, living in a place where no sky or tree leaves moved above her. And nothing seemed to disturb the scissor-tailed bird, not even the porchlight, one of my safeguards against unwanted visitors venturing at night down the dark, silent road, thinking it might lead to some pasture or abandoned house.

When I saw the nest was empty, I thought perhaps she had gone to search for food or for more materials for lining the nest. From where I stood, the nest seemed very shallow and I was always on the lookout for eggs, but never saw them.

But this was a deceptive nest, the inside soft, smooth, and deeper than it first appeared.

Before long, eggs opened and shells were tossed out to the ground for me to find, a chick probably exiting a place closed to me, their inner world invisible.

A door is a passage. It opens or it closes. She was at the door and living a life as quiet as mine, and active only when I was not there to see. Yet, through my human door, she found warmth and a woman who brought varieties of food, small pieces of fruit, maggots from the pasture, worms, seeds, all foods to see which she preferred.

All this time, inside were eggs with inner golden cells dividing invisibly. On the second day a heart began to beat; soon the beak formed and each part of the parent birds developed until the day, still invisible, they broke out, small pink creatures with no feathers, but soon becoming little feathered birds, all this in secret. No calling out. No looking over the edge, at least not while I watched. In some unknown way, they learned to fly as if it was in them to know their environment, had come to them genetically, along with the inherited history of flight. One day as I watched, three small birds flew immediately from the nest, looking like small adults, as if, for them, a single day of growth was like a biblical day. All I knew was that before this moment, in all my own watchful moments, I'd seen no infant birds, no eggs, no parents bringing food. They simply emerged all at once and joined the parent birds on the same branch of a nearby tree. All five on a single branch, the three young only slightly smaller.

Soon the magnetite in their brains, the pull of gravity and direction, constellations in the sky, would send them across the Gulf of Mexico to rain forests.

The paths above us, the flyways of the invisible, are in visibly endangered worlds, across latitudes and longitudes. Who would know if the places they live in part of the year would still be present and alive, ready for birds that return? Migrating to what is now the many nonexistent locations in what was once the tropical Southern wilds, places where DDT is still used.

In all that time I had never seen the male who watched over, present now. The kingbird flycatchers are monogamous birds. But I never saw the watching, never saw the young, as if always they waited for my absence or for night to begin first flight, if they did practice fledging. On the day the three little ones appeared, they did not need to learn flight. It was as if they were merely a smaller, fully competent, version of the parents who accompanied them on the branch, one parent bird on each end, prepared to protect their young.

They were another life who did not need me to watch over, but I had been enchanted by them. It was not the herbs I was supposed to have learned as a young woman, no tribal songs, the deer song of enchantment. No cantos. Nothing of the human mind. I thought of how long it took a parent bird to get one young crow just to leap from one branch to another. Of the foxes in a dark underground tunnel, all the beneath-earth lives, the once hidden wolves, the elk with its crown like an ancient garland announcing it was king.

Dear birds, I hope you consume many flies in the pasture before you leave without giving me notice, without saying *good-bye*. I am here. If fortunate, I will be here if one of you returns to the unkempt nest. Soft golden belly feathers. Orange beak and those dark liquid eyes. How could I not love you? I am a mere human being, slight in the world of all the other lives. Like your nest, there are depths in this world I do not know.

The Visitant

Everything is held in the silence of snow. Some of it drifts down the hills. Some climbs trees and walls. Some falls powerfully from the sky, water-heavy and so strongly, I expect to hear it touch the earth, but it is surprisingly silent. And some floats all directions in the sky alight, shining as crystals.

If the walls of the cabin could talk they would tell the story about how, all night as the weather continues, I drive the truck up and down the road, trying to keep it open until, finally tired, I leave the truck up on the main road, knowing the county plow may wall me in or cover the truck as the larger machine makes its own journeys back and forth. Hopefully I will be able to shovel out to drive on a plowed road.

I walk back home, stumbling through the bright heaviness, falling, wet and cold. It is a spring snow and I hope it is reaching its peak. Inside, from absolute exhaustion, I sleep, my long dark hair wet, spread across a pillow to dry.

It isn't long before I am awake, looking for warmer clothing, dressing quickly, seeing the tall mounds of frozen whiteness. It is cold in the bedroom that I call Siberia. It was originally added to the old cabin as a sunroom without insulation, only roofing shingles from the 1930s. I changed the siding, but it's still hardly insulated enough to keep the room warm, and now the small trees planted ninety years ago are tall and shade this part of the home daily as the sun passes west.

I am snowed into the valley and return to my earlier work, the labor of keeping a path open to the barn and from there to the horses. They have to eat more in this weather to keep their bodies warm. I have to keep up with the shoveling in order to feed "the girls." Fortunately, hay was recently delivered, this time by the brother of the girls who normally drive down my long narrow road. The girls wear chaps over their jeans and pile up the ton of hay in stacks too high for me to reach. I normally climb up on a ladder and toss down some bales. This time their brother delivered a few bales of alfalfa by accident.

If everything remains open, the food will last a long time. But it is also possible the snow will melt quickly and flood the storage area, wetting and molding the hay at the bottom and sides.

Keeping a path, I shovel the snow as high as possible to each side, then sweep it smooth with a broom. Through this walkway, I can carry out a large box of hay, then place it on a wide piece of cardboard to keep it from sinking into snow as the horses' warm breath melts it. This work will continue as long as snow falls.

Several hours later, while it's still light outside, I once again carry the large plastic box of hay to "the girls," again, worried about the arriving night cold. Turning a single corner, arms full of hay, I hear the huffing sound of a large animal's breath. Above the hay I see an elk, tall with great antlers. The hay is all the protection I have between us, the only safe thing, and I can carry it like a shield as snow silts around us.

We are two animals meeting and we stare at one another as if measuring our chances of surviving the startle of this unexpected meeting.

Me. I live in a human body, vulnerable. My hair is as long as the horse mane and matching like we are sister animals, but skin is the largest organ of this body and it seems too little, too thin. He stands large before me, thick winter fur, four great legs, hooves, and those enormous great antlers worn like a crown as if I should bow to him. Such majesty. Heavy to carry, I think, but easy weapons. He's at least nine hundred pounds to my hundred and he clatters his teeth as a warning, but I have to pass.

We are two different minds. Two species. Two ways of being. Two lives, both fragile for the moment, and neither of us able to even back up, move away from the other. We continue sizing up what we know of each other. To him, I could be a most dangerous animal. When humans appear, an elk often falls.

We live by different maps of this world. He reads land from a map I will never know, large and expansive with constant travels through the forest above and around us. Sometimes I see a herd or group at rest in the meadow up by the three apple trees where I occasionally pick and where his culture both gleans the ground and stands on hind legs to reach the apples high above. We have probably seen one another, but I do not know one from another. This boundary of not knowing stands between us as temporary fear. Perhaps all my unasked questions are the same he has, also unasked, as we stand inside the great snow wall of my making, blue-white, quiet and with darker blue crossing the sky, carrying one golden cloud.

I am a woman who lives small, gathering berries, planting, feeding other lives. The walls of the house are too small, close together, and there are days I long for more room. I travel shorter distances to the rural post office or next town for coffee with friends or for horse feed, the dog usually in back with her head out the window.

The golden elk exhales as if there is no choice but to survive with one another. I look down, not to appear a threat. I know enough about animals to avoid eye contact. Although some people stupidly want to look into their eyes as if reading another soul. I have often thought I would like to be part of a herd, elk or one of the smaller deer. I would like the luxurious life in green spring meadows, resting with others, eating the mosses, the wildflowers, the long sweet grasses near spring water that flows beneath willows. I would like to know more intimately the organism called an aspen grove that is truly all one plant. I want to sleep in a field with others for safety.

I have already seen that the hillsides above offer no escape for either of us, not with the large drifts of spring snow turned heavy, falling and shifting. How he reached this place is a mystery. No tracks or signs are visible in this world becoming silver. But then, wind would have blown new snow across any markings.

His teeth click as if he will bite. Perhaps he has forgotten the weapons on his head. I think a moment, then speak to him gently and walk past and back to the barn. His breath is white vapor. I go inside and grab some alfalfa left by accident and drop it in different places along the way, then glance back to see that he is eating. He is hungry, and otherwise, all he could eat is tree bark so I am grateful for the alfalfa since elk cannot eat the hay, while deer can't eat alfalfa. Also, I'm glad to protect surrounding trees and forest, though they are buried deep in snow, barely visible. I realize he does not cross over the snow. To do so may be dangerous and result in ice cuts, bleeding legs, or sinking into the great drifts that keep growing. So each time I feed horses, who are faring well except for falling ice on the mustang, I drop a bit of alfalfa here and there as if by mistake.

Waapiti. That is the word. Inside this word is the shade of fur lightening on the body toward the tail, also the pale belly. (The word may be a verb as well as a noun.)

By now the moon is full and white, encircled this night by a rainbow of color, a prism, all the roundness of different light outlined in shining red. It is called a moon dog, created by a halo of ice crystals about the moon.

As I sleep the snow falls. Twelve-foot drifts in the valley—I learn this only later by the measurements of others. Blue shadows outline the hills and diamond dust rises when wind lifts the new snow.

Each day we two animals learn a life together. It is a relationship, the only word that addresses this kind of connection, conveys the eventual lack of danger, and how two species new to one another learn to survive together. I feel, smell, and see his breath. He watches me move. This is part of how we speak. But his teeth still click together, as if to warn, *Do not come too close.* I ask permission each time I pass. I speak, look down, and pass around him as if the great antlers do not exist, and he allows the way.

The horses are there to be cared for and loved, always, and there is water to keep thawed and clean, a hose to drain. The snow on their backs is insulation. It's good for the winter coat one wears and for the other one who has the thick wild fur of her mustang self.

The human being is more than one kind of animal. Many stories and myths exist about aspects of the human being, including the two-faced god, one part that is kind, and one that carries the sword without regard for others, without considering damage or pain. That is a human being. I imagine the elk knows this about us. A hunting human may carry along the odor of a female elk in a bottle or spray, have a whistle that sounds like her call. There are many numbers of tricks. Most are from the side with the sword. How would an elk know which side they are meeting? Even a sixth sense can be wrong. No wonder they have fear and confusion. We lie and we cheat. Then, at times, humans want closeness or warmth. Whichever side is encountered will be the unanswered question all the while an elk is simply what it is. It wants to live. In its own fur, nothing is hidden. It watches. The female wants to protect the young. They love. They are careful to protect future generations.

The snow doesn't lessen, but different kinds fall. I study them while the shy dog, fearing the snow and elk, still barely goes very far from the door. We don't have enough words for the numerous kinds of snow, or for the ice that forms around the sides of the heated water tank. Crystal ice still freezes there in many shapes, all beautiful. Stalactites. Mountains of ice. We need as many names for snow as there are in parts of Alaska.

So much happens during the otherwise silent nights. More falls. Blue drifts of it move down from the above hills. Soon, branches break, overburdened with snow. Before long even the trees break, crashing down with the weight. Both of us listen to every breaking sound all night. The dog barks each time. I worry about which trees are falling and how close they are to the house. Then we are too tired, we cover ourselves and sleep.

Soon we have no electricity, although the electric panel down-stairs works and fortunately it keeps the horses' water thawed. I worry about two trees in a perfect position to fall on us as the world covers itself with hoarfrost.

When morning light returns, I make more coffee, grateful electricity will heat water downstairs, otherwise uninhabitable.

Waapiti: Those whose fur lightens. Tecumseh, the prophet who tried to unite our tribes on the eastern side of the continent, called the elk *ghosts of the high country*. In this high country one ghost has found a human, finding safety and nurturing. Maybe it isn't rare in this location, since before hunting season each year herds arrive in the town above us to find safety from the hunters. Elk sit on the lawns of those who live there, finding rich grasses that remain from summer. Some cross the highway and everyone stops. Tourists take photos. And often, they are at the upper bend in our dirt road where three apple trees are aging.

It is still an early dark, indigo, when I go out to feed horses. The elk is also waiting, so for him I drop alfalfa. On my way back, I look for the moon. It is no longer in the sky. I also wait for the snow to sublime, to become dry and form space between the smallest particles of snow that will evaporate. Then some rises to the sky and the rest, if touched, falls into minute bits. It creates a sound, the music of crystal, or at least it is what I could hear. Some say there is no sound but that is also true of the northern lights. Some hear them. Others can't even measure the sound with their instruments, but no one doubts the many who say the world has its music.

Falling into the rhythm of earth, nights never have the feeling of being alone. They are a richness of silence. The silence is a kind of poetry. I take out my finest paper, my best pen, and slowly, carefully, begin to write. I write, read, sleep. Outside is the low and quiet of clouds.

I think often of the words of poetry and silence. The words already exist where wind wrote on the snow. Now it writes across the surface of snow moving like a dune of sand, rippling, constantly changing, speaking. The poet laureate of Alaska, John Haines, comes to mind. His winter words. But words are breath, wind, air, what we all share. I cannot help but appreciate the beauty of the elk, ghost of the high country, with his own fog of breath. The elegant antlers remind me of those in ancient cave art with their grace hidden in the darkness. He becomes one of inner earth, and every move is one of grace.

Grace is natural with animals and with some few people. There are those who have it and who move without any encumbrance of our species, our burdens. While most other species have bypassed awkwardness, they have also spent lifetimes traveling together without effort or judgment or self-consciousness. Those qualities belong to us. Animal grace is natural, and the elk has pure animal grace, the grace that knows who and what he is.

One day I hear human voices, an alien sound. A rescue team has come down to see if anyone here needs help. The electric box is pulled off the wall because of a broken tree, and it is alive on the snow. The person who noticed it worked for the electric company and knew how to place it all back on the wall. It is a surprise that no one had been electrocuted. The moisture of snow and ice could have carried live electricity. They asked if everything else was all right. I said I'd gotten by with wood and the electricity downstairs. It was not an emergency. They see all the broken trees surrounding my home and what good fortune that the house had not been hit. The trees I thought might fall on the house each broke in half and fell on different sides. They tell me how lucky I am, and they don't see the elk.

Once the silence has been broken, human voices invaded, untouched snow now walked across, the human presence has brought the world back into this canyon. It is now that I make the path. I use snowshoes and weigh down the sled with bricks to make the trail to the road where my truck is snowed in, hopefully not covered by snow from the plow. After much labor, I shovel it out, heavy snow moved away, and as always, the old farm truck starts. I'm able to drive me to town where I can purchase food and stop at the hardware store for salt and sand for the shining dark ice that comes after the beginning of snowmelt. I stop on the way home to visit a friend who also lives alone but has a short walk to her place. By the time I park and walk home, it is dark.

On the path, the elk and I meet one another in a new place. It's a moonless night. He stands on the passage I made. It holds his weight. In all his antlered glory, he still clicks his teeth at me. I tell him I need to pass by, and he permits a very close passage.

This is the last time I see him, at least that I know of. I didn't count how many days we were in that one walkway together, but I will always imagine him walking out on that path, alone, up the road in the icy darkness, probably to find the others in his herd.

I think of his large beauty often, whenever I see a herd, when it snows, or in autumn, when I hear elk bugling. I always wonder if one of them is the one who I have lived with.

I lived for a countless time, as Tecumseh said, with a ghost of the high country.

Watching Over

This land, I watch over it,
the place with ancient stories,
the plants of medicine,
the place where mountain lions
walk down the hill and look in on the light of my life

in this little cabin made of happiness,
of stone laid on stone so perfectly
a hundred years ago,
the year before my father was born.

The bison is now down in the valley
filled with great trees,
down near the quartz shining
in veins through dark earth.

The fireplace is made of that quartz,
some with crystals bright in firelight,
and pushed into the mortar, the single baby tooth
of the one new child.

In this valley of trees and river and crystal,
the fault lines of history broke.

Now something always watches over
this small cabin, the bison away from its herd,

the ghostly wolves that passed
outside the door last year,
the great hawk flying across
and even the fox that sits each morning

and looks in for no other reason
than to watch how I live,
to make sure it is
        the right way.

ACKNOWLEDGMENTS

 Many friendships have kindled my creative life for many years. They are friends who have listened to my stories about animals, insects, the appearance of certain birds, or the best manner of pasture planting. They have worried about our snowstorms. Or best, have met me for coffee, a film, a field trip on days I might escape from chores. These include long friendships with Marilyn Auer and her offerings of books; Kathleen Cain, who knows the names of everything I find; Becky and Joe Hogan, who have read every book of worth; Barbara Roubidoux and Rudy the rooster; Debra Jang, who also loves grandchildren; and my own loved grandchildren, Danielle Griffith and Cami Griffith, often sharing with me conversations about the same complete love of the world around us, the same grief, and too little time together. Of course, I adore and admire their talented artist mother, Kathy McGaa Griffith, and I will always have great and forever mother love for Tanya Thunder Horse.

Deborah Miranda and Margo Solod, I love you so much for your intelligence, help, and for being St. Nicholas. We are friends for life. I have gratitude for Brenda Peterson with her seabird calls, her love of animal lives, and our friendship centered on those lives. Love to Pam Uschuk for so much support and for our long conversations. Her words have inspired. For Linda Rodriquez who has often spoken with me about healing and writing.

Many thanks to dear friend Karen Oser, for giving me a day off each week, and for caring.

Thank you to Dale Peterson, one originator of the Thoreau Nature Writing Awards and a brilliant thinker and writer of animal life and history, especially in the Gombe research crew.

With gratitude and friendship to those who are my nearest neighbors, Chris and Ciara, who have opened this road more than once and been mealtime friends and visitors; to David and Rita Greenberg/Davito, arriving at the top of the road to clear the way in. I'm grateful for my friend with whom I've wandered these hills and also worked with at the Birds of Prey Foundation. Thanks, Ricardo Salas, for repairing the fence that strangers cut down.

My very special appreciation to Helene Atwan for the great kindnesses offered as this book evolved, for believing in the work, and to Haley Lynch for her always perfect ideas about the shape of the book, and to Susan Lumenello for the difficult final job of careful reading and editing. All three have devoted time and attention to this book.

Thanks so much to Louis Roe for his wonderful cover and interior design for the book, and to Kim Arney for creating the interior. And special thanks to the Chickasaw Nation's artist in residence, James Blackburn, for his elegant cover and interior illustrations.

My heart is always open to Larry Henderson, brother who shares my love of other-than-human lives, an amazing wildlife photographer who did a perfect photo of this wild human!

As always, with special gratitude to David Curtis who has been here for me and for his love of the animal household.

Without the great amount of time offered me by the Mesa Refuge and Susan Tillett and the rest of the board, this book might not have been finished. Also, my heart is with the Native Arts and Culture Foundation and others who have given me such gracious support over the years.